Z/28

A SOURCE BOOK

EDITED AND ANNOTATED BY

Joe Collins

Motorbooks International
Publishers & Wholesalers Inc
Osceola, Wisconsin 54020, USA

Bookman Publishing/Baltimore, Maryland

Printed in the U.S.A.
Copyright 1984 in U.S.A. by Bookman Dan!, Inc.

ISBN 0-934780-36-6

First Edition
First Printing

Inquiries may be directed to:
Bookman Dan!, Inc.
P.O. Box 13492
Baltimore, Maryland 21203

Book trade distribution by:
Motorbooks International
P. O. Box 2
Osceola, Wisconsin 54020

Contents

To "uncle" Bob Parks, who started my love affair
with cars when I was four, and to Paul Muse, who
first gave me the opportunity to write about them.

Preface

Vincent W. Piggins can be called the father of the Z/28. It was he who met with SCCA officials to help make the race-intended Camaro eligible for Trans Am competition. He also sold then-new Chevrolet General Manager Pete Estes on the idea of racing and winning by showing him a prototype equipped with a high-performance version of the 283 V-8. And it was he again who suggested mating the 327 block with the 283 crankshaft to obtain the 302 cubic inch displacement, just under the 305 limit set by the SCCA. Through the efforts of Vince Piggins, Chevrolet had a successful challenger to the competition Mustangs that had been cleaning up at the tracks — the Z/28.

Selection of the name was purely serendipity. In a hurry to name the prototype before showing the car, someone noticed that the order number for the option was RPO (Regular Production Option) Z-28 and suggested they use it. A quick consensus was achieved and the Z/28 was born. It has become one of the most popular high-performance ponycars ever built.

The purpose of a Source Book is to tell the story of a car through the original manufacturer's literature, some of which, certainly in the case of the Camaro, may be quite rare. In each chapter, the front covers of the items used during this book's research are shown in a montage on the first Source Book page and then the important pages from those brochures are reproduced on the following Source Book pages (and keyed in the text at the beginning of each chapter).

The '67 Super Sports by Chevrolet

The Camaro was introduced in 1967, but unless you were a real car aficionado, you would not have known about the Z/28 option. Even most Chevrolet salesmen didn't know about it. None of the sales literature for that year mentioned or illustrated that now-famous Regular Production Option (RPO) number. The big advertising push was on the Super Sport and the Rally Sport trim package. That was the way Chrevolet wanted it; they didn't feel the Z/28 was appropriate for the street. Most of the 1967 Zs went to dealers or individuals who intended to put them on the track, because that's where Chevrolet wanted to show the world that the Camaro was not just a GM copy of the Mustang.

To get a Z/28 in 1967, you had to go in and practically walk the salesman through the order sheet. What you ordered was a base Camaro (model 12337), which listed for $2,466. Then you checked off RPO Z-28 for $400.25. But that wasn't all; you also had to order the mandatory front disc brakes with power assist (J-56), a $100.10 option and the Muncie four-speed manual transmission with 2.20:1 low, which was another $184.00. So the minimum list for a Z/28 was $3,150.35; what you paid depended on the deal you could strike. Above that, you could order almost any option, as long as it didn't conflict with the Z/28 package. What you specifically could not order were the SS package, automatic transmission, air conditioning, or the convertible body. This car was meant for serious drivers only.

The Z/28 package included the following items: F-41 handling suspension, Corvette 15x6 inch Rally wheels fitted with 7.35-15 Goodyear tires, 24:1 ratio manual steering, the now-famous dual wide stripes running from cowl to grille and from rear window to trunk lip and, of course, the 302 engine.

The 302 engine was derived by mating the 327 block with the 283 crankshaft. It was fitted with the Corvette L-69 big-port heads, a baffled oil pan, a high-pressure oil pump, solid lifters and a camshaft with 346 degrees duration for both intake and exhaust. A 780-800 cfm Holley carburetor fed the cylinders through a tuned aluminum intake manifold. For appearance, the engine had chromed valve covers and air cleaner (open type), plus a bright oil filler tube and cap. The compression ratio was 11:1. Horsepower was listed as 290, but that was just an arbitrary number. True power ratings were never established by Chevrolet. It was suggested in many

car magazines at the time that power was much higher, perhaps as much as 100 horsepower more.

A single exhaust, fed by cast-iron exhaust manifolds, was standard from the factory, but headers, along with intake manifolds and carburetors, were available as options. These items came in the trunk, to be installed by the dealer or mechanically-inclined purchaser. Significantly, Chevrolet didn't flinch at warranting the Z/28; it carried the same 2-year/24,000-mile warranty as the rest of the Camaros.

All 1967 Camaros were fitted with single-leaf rear springs with the rear shocks mounted just ahead of the rear axle. This configuration caused the high-powered Z/28 and SS models to suffer tremendous axle tramp under heavy acceleration.

Z/28 sales paled when compared to the heavily promoted SS model. Besides having a bigger engine, 350 cubic inches and 295 horsepower (and later, 396 cubic inches and 325 horses), the SS could be ordered with an automatic transmission and air conditioning, plus it could be had in convertible as well as coupe form. Not being able to get these features on the Z/28 certainly had to limit its appeal to the public.

The Rally Sport package was a popular appearance option. The most noticeable feature was the disappearing headlights, which were concealed behind doors that matched the grille and swivelled toward the center when the lights were in use. The front turn signals were mounted below the bumper instead of in the grille. The taillights were all red instead of the half-red/half-clear style used on the base model, with the backup lights mounted below the rear bumper. Chrome lower body side molding (with a blacked-out rocker panel on some colors), color-keyed pinstripes along the upper body crease, wheel well lip mors were available on the Z/28, as were both the standard and custom interior trims.

A total of 220,917 1967 Camaros were built. The SS models accounted for 34,411 units; only 602 were Z/28s.

The main 1967 Camaro catalogue was an over-size item (see pages 8-13), the only such over-size item Camaro would have until the last year considered in this book—1981. The Camaro SS was prominently featured in the large Chevy sports department folder (see page 15). Various Camaro-related mailers appear on pages 14 and 16-20. A Camaro Pace Card over-size color postcard appears on page 20, bottom.

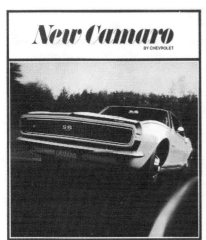

New Camaro

WIDE STANCE STABILITY AND BIG-CAR POWER KEYNOTE THIS EXCITING NEW ROAD MACHINE FROM CHEVROLET

Wide-footed stability that's built in gives Camaro a road-clutching tenacity. With this exceptional wide stance (only an inch shy of five feet front and rear) the new Camaro rides like much larger cars. In the handling department, the favorable ratio of wide stance tread to wheelbase gives it clinging power on curves, incredible straight-line tracking.

Camaro is band-box new by Chevrolet, and a freshly styled example of how fine an exciting road machine can look. Both models —convertible and sport coupe—have the long sports-car-inspired hood. The body styling sweeps your eye astern. And from the rear, Camaro's stylistic freshness sets it apart from the mundane.

By now it's clear that Camaro is a go as well as a show machine. Camaro offers you the kind of deep breathing big cubic-inch power you might expect only in far larger cars—topped by a 350-cubic-inch V8 that's exclusively Camaro's. Also in the power line-up: standard 140-hp six-cylinder or 210-hp V8. You can specify a 155-hp six (with larger displacement) or a 275-hp 327-cu.-in. V8. Full details on power teams will be found on pages 14-15.

Camaro hosts all of the 1967 standard safety features including dual master cylinder brake system, GM-developed energy-absorbing steering column and passenger-guard door locks. For the complete list of all standard safety items, see page 13.

You can put yourself into the Camaro you see pictured on pages 4-5. Or you can specify the Rally Sport version illustrated on pages 6-7. Perhaps you want to order the SS 350 excitingly spelled out on pages 8-9. If you like, you can even combine the verve of the SS 350 with the striking Rally Sport version, as shown at right. Dressing up the interior is an adventure, too. Check the Custom Interior on pages 10-11 for special luxury on order.

Do you want to personalize your machine to say "you" all over? Then you'll want to look over all of the Options and Custom Features detailed on pages 16 and 17. For instance, you can order a brand new Chevrolet-Delco Stereo Tape System that includes a special 80-minute tape program narrated by Lorne Greene of *Bonanza*. Or specify stereo tape and AM/FM radio with FM stereo for true sonic enjoyment. And to round out the comfort idea, Four-Season air conditioning. Other Options: vinyl roof, 4-Speed, Strato-ease headrests, special instrumentation and a Sports Console—in short, all you could want to individualize your Camaro.

You're witnessing, on the pages of this catalog, a true *command performance*! You've been waiting for a Chevrolet like this . . . now it's here!

Individualizing your Camaro is fun. Look over the extra-cost Options and Custom Features you can order on pages 16-17 and throughout the text and illustrations in this catalog.

Shown on front cover: SS 350 Camaro Sport Coupe in Butternut Yellow with Rally Sport option and black vinyl roof cover you can order.

Copyright 1966, Chevrolet Motor Division, General Motors Corporation

Shown above: SS 350 Camaro Sport Coupe in Bolero Red with Rally Sport option and black vinyl roof cover you can specify.

Rally Sport Camaro

FROM HIDEAWAY HEADLIGHTS TO UNIQUE TAILLIGHTS THIS CAMARO SAYS SWINGER FROM ALL ANGLES!

Specifying the Rally Sport Camaro really does electrifying things to the appearance. You get: "rs" emblems on the grille and going away on the fuel filler cap; full-width, black lattice grille with concealed headlights; lower body side molding; black accent below body side molding (with certain colors); color-keyed body accent stripes; sporty styling for parking/turning lights in front; sports-styled backup lights; and distinctive edged-in-black taillight treatment with two lamps in each

taillight unit for driving, braking and turn signal indication.

In addition to these outside eye-pleasers, you get bright metal front and rear wheel opening moldings, plus a bright drip gutter molding on sport coupes. Inside, an "rs" emblem appears on the steering wheel center.

What's the result when you're all through ordering your Rally Sport? You've fitted your Camaro with the action look that proclaims to all your exceptional trim selection.

Any of a host of power team combinations is available for your Rally Sport Camaro. You can have a Rally Sport Camaro with the standard 140-hp Turbo-Thrift 230 six-cylinder engine or 210-hp Turbo-Fire 327 standard V8. Specify another 327-cubic-inch V8 with a four-barrel carburetor and 275 hp if you like. The choice—and fun—is yours.

Personalizing your Camaro is one of life's more pleasant experiences. Check the list on pages 16-17 for items you can order; many items are also covered in text and illustrations throughout the catalog.

Open and shut case—concealed headlight system on Rally Sport Camaros. Grille sections blend when headlight is concealed for smooth, unbroken look.

Distinctive rear styling with twin-unit taillight assemblies edged in black, backup lights below bumper and "rs" emblem on fuel filler cap.

Rally Sport Camaro instrument panel in blue. Note "rs" emblem on horn button.

Rally Sport Camaro Convertible in Granada Gold.

SS 350 Camaro

THE GO MACHINE LOOK OUTSIDE TELLS EVERYONE YOU'VE GOT THE NEW 350 V8 INSIDE!

Maybe the Camaro in standard measure has caught your fancy . . . or possibly you've decided to deck one out as a Rally Sport. But what you really want now is a goer as well—and one that looks like a goer. Then the SS 350 Camaro is what you should specify. The looks outside tell all what you've got inside—the exciting new 350-cu.-in. V8.

Here's what lets admirers in on the story: unique color-keyed hood striping plus simulated louvers on the hood. "SS" letters on the fenders tell the knowledgeable that you have the go machine that's all business. "SS 350" emblem in the grille. And those who get

the stern view (there'll be many) will have to look quickly to spot the "SS 350" emblem on the fuel filler cap. Inside, too: "SS 350" emblem appears with authority in the steering wheel center. SS 350 models are appropriately shod with red stripe tires.

You get the big inch V8 in SS 350, too. An authoritative new 350-cubic-inch V8 topped by a four-barrel carburetor and vented by dual exhausts for 295 horsepower. Specify the SS 350 Camaro in either convertible or sport coupe form. And for dress inside, turn the page and scan the Custom Interior shown there. Imagine what an SS 350 would look

like if you ordered it with Rally Sport equipment. Want to? You can! And with the Custom Interior, the SS 350 is boldest!

Not only do you get the going looks and the big V8, you can also specify disc brakes for the front wheels. The dual master cylinder brake system utilizes drum brakes on the rear wheels and includes a proportioning valve to distribute braking effort to front and rear wheels for even, sure stops.

Personalizing your Camaro is one of life's more pleasant experiences. Check the list on pages 16-17 for items you can order; many items are also covered in text and illustrations throughout the catalog.

"SS 350" emblem adorns the center of the steering wheel.

Unique hood striping sets off the SS 350's looks.

"SS 350" emblem on fuel filler cap.

Gleaming hood trim on SS 350 tops the big 295-hp V8.

SS 350 Camaro Convertible in Ermine White with Rally Sport option you can order.

hoist the hood of Chevrolet's command performance car:
CAMARO

If it's the SS version of the swinging new Camaro, you'll say: "WOW! Look at that 325-hp Turbo-Jet 396 V8." No need to say anything else. As one who has experienced the capability of Chevrolet engines, you'll be impressed with this just-released Camaro engine as well as the fact it is available with the three-speed Turbo Hydra-Matic transmission, among others. And because the personal-size Camaro, with its short-deck, long-hood styling, is brand new, you really have to see both sport coupe and convertible to appreciate what you can do with them. You can stack Camaro any way you want. Basically, it offers Chevrolet's engineering excellence, Body by Fisher craftsmanship, all the new safety features, handling and ride superiority. After that it's up to you. You can be a purist and take it the way it is. Or dress it up the Rally Sport way. Or maybe you'll go for the spirit of the SS version. Some put both Rally Sport and SS together. Whichever way you go, the results will be an exciting road machine that distinctively reflects your personal tastes.

SS 350 Camaro Convertible with Rally Sport Option in Bolero Red

Camaro SS 350

Mechanical features

295-hp Turbo-Fire 350 V8. Entirely new engine, exclusive with Camaro SS 350 (see chart at right for specs). Provides big-car power that complements Camaro's wide-stanced tread. High-strength thinwall castings. 1.94"-dia. intake valves, 1.50"-dia. exhaust valves. Valve lift: .3900" inlet, .4100" exhaust. Inlet valves open 36° BTC, close 94° ABC. Exhausts open 86° BTC, close 54° ABC. Inlet 310°, exhaust 320° duration. Special suspension components included with SS 350.

Transmissions

3-Speed fully synchronized. Standard transmission with the 350 V8. Gear ratios: 2.54:1 first, 1.50:1 second, 1.00:1 third, 2.63:1 reverse. Column shift. Extra-cost special version: 2.41:1 first, 1.57:1 second, 1.00:1 third, 2.41:1 reverse. Floor shift.

4-Speed fully synchronized. Extra-cost. Ratios: 2.52:1 first, 1.88:1 second, 1.47:1 third, 1.00:1 fourth, 2.59:1 reverse. Chrome-plated floor-mounted shift lever.

Powerglide automatic. Extra cost. Two-speed, three-element automatic transmission. Ratios 3.70:1 to 1.76:1 range. Column shift lever, floor-mounted when Sports Console is specified.

Appearance features

Exterior. Distinctive hood treatment with contrasting color bands and simulated louvers. "SS 350" emblems in grille and on fuel filler cap. "SS" letters on front fenders. Slender bright molding on body sills. Red-stripe tires (white-stripe available) on 14" x 6" wheels and hub caps.

Style Trim Group. Specifying these items adds front and rear wheel opening moldings, color-keyed body accent stripes and, on sport coupes, a drip gutter molding.

Rally Sport. Outstanding exterior appearance design you can order for your SS 350. Includes, plus items in Style Trim Group, full-width black grille with concealed headlights, parking lights relocated below bumper, wide lower body molding, distinctive taillights edged in black, back-up lights relocated below bumper, distinctive emblems and, depending on color, black paint below body side molding.

Custom Interior. May also be ordered for SS 350. Includes seven color-keyed all-vinyl interiors, accent bands on front bucket and conventional rear seats, special door trim with integral armrest, recessed door release and carpeted scuff panel. Oval steering wheel with SS center emblem. Circular courtesy lights on rear roof quarters in sport coupe, under instrument panel in convertible. Here's another personalizing extra available when Custom Interior is specified: Stratoback front seat (replacing buckets) with fold-down center armrest—in three colors and accent band combinations.

Special Interior. Also available for SS 350. Includes bright trimmed pedal pads—accelerator, brake, clutch and parking brake. Windshield pillar moldings and roof rail moldings (on sport coupe).

Extra-cost items. Stereo tape system, AM/FM radio with FM stereo, Four-Season air conditioning, Sports Console, special instrumentation, Strato-ease headrests, fold-down rear seat in sport coupe, vinyl roof in black or beige, power windows, steering and brakes, Soft-Ray tinted glass, shoulder belts for front seat passengers, Comfortilt steering wheel, power-operated convertible top, wheel trim covers, simulated wire or Mag-style wheel covers, rear seat speaker, deck lid luggage carrier, ski carrier, door edge guards, Tri-volume horn. Also Strato-back front seat, rubber cushion bumper guards, Cruise-Master speed control, remote control outside rearview mirror, wood-grained plastic steering wheel, rear antenna, front disc brakes, sintered-metallic drum brake linings, deep-tone exhaust system, temperature-controlled fan, heavy-duty radiator, 12-42 amp. Delcotron and special steering, plus many more. Check your Chevrolet dealer for full details.

Interior dimensions

	Sport Coupe		Convertible	
	Front	Rear	Front	Rear
Head room	37.4"	36.5"	37.4"	36.8"
Leg room	41.8"	31.5"	42.5"	29.6"
Shoulder room	56.8"	53.8"	56.7"	47.3"
Usable luggage space (cubic feet)		8.25		5.6

SS 350 engine (RPO 148) specifications

Engine type	Valve-in-head V8
Displacement (cu.-in.)	350
Bore and stroke	4.0" x 3.48"
Horsepower @ RPM	295 @ 4800
Torque @ RPM	380 @ 3200
Compression ratio	10.25:1
Carburetion	Four-barrel/automatic choke
Camshaft	General performance
Valve lifters	Hydraulic
Exhaust system	Dual with resonators

ENGINE	TRANSMISSION	OPTION NO. (RPO)	REAR AXLE		TRANSMISSION	OPTION NO. (RPO)	REAR AXLE	
			STANDARD	OPTIONAL			STANDARD	OPTIONAL
295-hp Turbo-Fire 350 V8	3-Speed	STD.	3.31:1	3.07:1 3.55:1	4-Speed	M20	3.31:1	3.07:1, 3.55:1 3.73:1, 4.10:1*, 4.56:1*, 4.88:1*
	Special 3-Speed	M13	3.31:1	3.07:1, 3.55:1* 3.73:1, 4.10:1* 4.56:1*, 4.88:1*	Powerglide	M35	3.31:1	3.07:1, 3.55:1, 3.73:1

*Positraction required; available with all other ratios.

Camaro Convertible with Rally Sport option

like nothing you've ever driven before

Can we change your life in 20 minutes? No, but we think we can change your driving preference. Let me put you in a Camaro by Chevrolet and the rest is up to you. Chances are you'll find yourself becoming so quickly attached to the looks, the luxury, the ride and the performance that you'll never want to go back to ordinary driving again. You've never driven a car like this before simply because there's never been a car like this before. Like to chance it?

Come in and drive one or I'll bring one to you
Just call me!

GO camaro by Chevrolet

IT'LL DRIVE YOU ABSOLUTELY
MOD

What's so special about Camaro? Check the lean form, the curving profile, the newly tucked-tail design. Look inside. Front buckets, wall-to-wall carpeting, vinyl (all-around) are all standard fare. From there—you're on your own. Take the Camaro in standard measure or MOD-ify it to suit your individual taste. There's the Rally Sport option, the SS 350 package or a swinging combination of both. Five great engines are yours for the choosing from the spirited 140-hp. Six to the SS 350-cu. incher. Custom interiors, too, plus a host of options and custom features to add or subtract at slightest whim.

When you sum it all up, there's only one thing you *can't* get with Camaro—bored!

1967

For young

Fasten your belts and get away from wall to wall dle of safety features—like dual master cylinder b

Step in. Strap up. Step out—in Camaro from Chevrolet. Track assuredly through corners and curves, hug the road on the straightaway on Camaro's new wide tread stance to wheelbase ratio. Ride easily on husky coil springs up front; Mono-Plate leaf springs in rear. Camaro's got a suspension second to none that spells sure-footed stability with a capital "SS". And you can get an extra measure of performance with such available extras as front disc brakes, positraction axle ratios, special 3-speed, 4-speed and Powerglide transmissions, manual or power fast steering and special-purpose front and rear suspension. Whichever body style or engine you choose, from five distinct breeds, you're in for a thrilling experience—instant obedience.

You don't just drive a Camaro you command it!

18

people of all ages

boredom in a big hurry. Everything about Camaro from roof to road says "have a go at it!" And wrapped up inside is a bun-aking system, GM-developed energy-absorbing steering column, four-way hazard warning flasher and more—all standard.

You can get as much Camaro as you can handle*

Start with a brace of buckets up-front, carpeting underfoot, all-vinyl interior and where you go from there is strictly up to you. Twenty-four exterior-interior combinations are yours for the ordering. Add the Rally Sport package with special trim and hideaway headlamps. Heap on a few other goodies like vinyl roof, stereo tape system, special instrumentation, fold-down rear seat. Go completely MOD—take 'em all! That's the great thing about Camaro from Chevrolet.

*\$2,466⁰⁰ Manufacturer's suggested retail price. Camaro Sport Coupe, model 12337. All prices include federal excise tax and suggested dealer delivery and handling charge. Transportation charges, accessories, other optional equipment, state and local taxes additional.

BIG SAVINGS DURING
OUR CAMARO PACESETTER SALE!

Now's your chance for real big savings on a specially equipped Camaro. You get extras like these at special savings.

Full Wheel Covers	155-hp Turbo-Thrift 6
Deluxe Steering Wheel	Extra Interior Trim
Whitewall Tires	Wheel Opening Moldings
Body Side Striping	Special Hood Stripe
Front and Rear Bumper Guards	

Other savings available on power steering and power brakes, Powerglide transmission or, if you prefer, a floor-mounted shift lever (with standard 3-speed transmission).

Come in and take a trial run in a Pacesetter —the great 1967 Camaro. And look at all the '67 Chevrolets while you're here.

Camaro Sport Coupe   Camaro Convertible

YOUR CHEVY SALESMAN

Very few cosmetic changes were made to the Camaro for 1968. The body remained the same, but the grille now emphasized a horizontal motif using argent accenting. Vent windows were dropped with the advent of flow-through ventilation and the grilles on non-RS models sported rectangular turn signals instead of the round lenses of the previous year. To comply with new federal safety regulations, side-marker lights were mounted just behind the front and just ahead of the rear bumpers. However, the most significant change for 1968 wasn't cosmetic. Multi-leaf rear springs replaced the single-leaf units on V-8 equipped models and the rear shock absorbers were now staggered; one shock was mounted ahead of the rear axle and one behind it. These two changes significantly reduced the axle tramp problem that had afflicted the high-performance Camaros the previous year.

The Z/28 option still carried the same restrictions: no convertible, no automatic transmission and no air conditioning. Front disc brakes with power assist and a four-speed transmission were still mandatory options. Three four-speeds were available for 1968: the standard model, a heavy-duty version with the same ratios as the standard model and the unit from the L-88 (350 cid engine).

Again, Chevrolet did not mention the Z/28 in the brochures, but they did promote it in the enthusiast magazines, stimulating a lot more demand for this model. The successes on the Trans Am circuit also boosted buyer interest, especially when Camaro took the championship that season.

Z/28s were easier to identify in 1968; "Z/28" or "302" emblems were mounted on the front fenders to accompany the twin wide stripes on the hood and trunk. Again the Z could be had in base or Rally Sport form and in any of the 15 colors offered. Interior colors were dropped from eight to six choices and could be had in standard or custom trim.

The SS model continued to be more popular than the Z/28. It could be ordered with either the 295 hp 350 or the 325 hp 396 engines and teamed with three- or four-speed manual or with the three-range Turbo Hydramatic transmission. The SS Camaros could also be had in convertible form and equipped with air conditioning, further broadening its appeal over the Z/28.

The Rally Sport option continued its popularity in 1968. It still featured the disappearing headlamps, with the turn signals mounted under the front bumper. The taillights changed to two-piece red lenses, with the backup lights mounted under the rear bumper. Chrome lower body side moldings, wheel well lip moldings and drip rail moldings (on coupes) were included. On non-SS models, "RS" emblems were mounted in the center of the grille, on the gas cap and on the horn ring. Instead of "RS" emblems on the front fender like the previous year, the words "rally sport" were spelled out in lower-case chrome letters between the front wheel wells and the doors.

Of 235,151 Camaros made for 1968, 7,199 were Z/28s. The heavily-promoted SS models accounted for 27,844 units.

The main Camaro catalogue for 1968 was smaller than in the previous year, but no less attractive (see pages 22-28). A sheet on the mid-year "Customized" Camaro model appears on page 29. A magazine ad for the Z/28 option appears on page 30. The various Camaro-related items used during research on this book appear in the montage below.

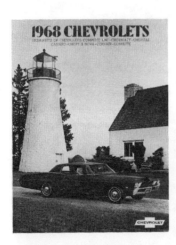

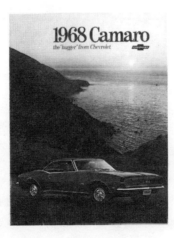

Rally Sport Package

Now that you're acquainted with the 1968 Camaro, you should be properly conditioned to take a look at one of the more glamorous versions you can order . . . the Rally Sport. If you have a weakness for elegance, you'll be a pushover for this one . . . in coupe or convertible.

Take the Rally Sport's concealed headlights, for instance. Where else can you find them at these prices?

Are you performance-minded? So is this one. That solid-going wide stance should give you a clue. Then see its whole impressive array of power team combina- tions in the chart on Page 15. For now, be informed that even the standard 230-cubic-inch Turbo-Thrift 140-hp Six or the 327-cubic-inch 210-hp V8 is a sprightly performer. But if your power requirements are different, you're sure to find just the engine that pleases you among Camaro's selection of sixes and V8's.

Other Rally Sport features underscore its individuality. Among them, wheel opening moldings and "RS" emblems on grille and fuel filler cap. Can't mistake this car's personality. It's a standout.

Camaro Convertible with Rally Sport equipment you can order

Camaro SS Package

It's to the fun crowd that we dedicate the Camaro SS. A husky performer and looks it. Beefed-up suspension system and 350-cubic-inch V8 engine (you can order a 396-cubic-inch V8, too).

You can spot a Camaro SS by the raised simulated air intake on the hood and distinctive front accent band around the grille. Camaro SS means not only superb performance but roadability to match. Other identifying marks: "SS" emblems front, side and rear; red stripe wide-oval tires. Farther on, we tell you about some of the good things underneath. What's that you say? You'd like an SS with all the features that come on a Rally Sport. Easiest thing in the world. Just specify both—and get both on the same car. It's as easy as that.

Unless otherwise specified, your Camaro SS comes with a standard interior like the one you saw on page 5. But on any Camaro you can specify the Special Interior Group with deluxe accents. These accents also are included in Custom Interior.

Camaro SS Sport Coupe

Order your Camaro as a Rally Sport or an SS. Here

Rally Sport
Rally Sport features in brief: • Concealed headlights • Special full-width grille • Parking and direction signal lights mounted below front bumper • "RS" emblem on grille • Back-up lights below bumper • "RS" emblem on gas filler cap • Lower body side molding • "Rally Sport" script on front fender • Roof drip molding on sport coupe • Wheel opening moldings • Belt molding.

Camaro SS
Camaro SS features in brief: • Raised simulated air intake on special hood (stack-type with 396-cu.-in. V8) • "SS" grille emblem • Special hood insulation and chassis components • 350- or 396-cubic-inch V8 engine • Color-keyed front accent band (black with light colors; white with darker colors) • "SS" identification on front fender and fuel filler cap • Red (or white) stripe wide-oval tires • Black rear panel with 396-cubic-inch engine • Multi-leaf rear springs.

are the details.

Here are the facts about how and why the Camaro

Chassis and Mechanical Features

Body-frame—Unitized all-welded steel body construction with a separate front rubber-mounted frame section that provides extra strength and support.

Body construction — Rugged body components are used throughout to increase strength and rigidity. Cross-braced bow-like members in the sport coupe roof add firm support, while the convertible has rocker panels of heavier gauge steel to lend extra stiffness to the convertible design.

Body protection—Camaro is built with an eye to long, long life. Galvanized members are used along with other rust preventive materials. We even go so far as to put fenders inside the outer fenders to shield against corrosion from salt, slush, snow and ice. Rocker panels are the flush-and-dry design. Rain and snow water entering the vents at cowl level wash out the rocker panel while incoming air dries it.

Roadability and suspension—Camaro rests on a 108-inch wheelbase with 59.0-inch tread front and 58.9-inch rear—wide stance for flat, level cornering and solid going on the straightaway. A combination of independent coil spring suspension up front and Mono-Plate single leaf springs at the rear provide just the right balance between smoothness and firmness. Special multi-leaf rear springs with extra-cost V8s (with 4-Speed transmission only with 275-hp 327 V8). Bias-mounted rear shock absorbers offer improved suspension control.

Brakes—Safety-Master self-adjusting brakes give you a full 168.9 square inches of bonded lining area. Brakes have dual master cylinder with warning light on instrument panel. Rayon-reinforced front and rear brake hoses. All brake lines are corrosion-resistant. Parking brake is foot-operated with fingertip release.

Exhaust system—Highly corrosion-resistant for long life. Exhaust emission control system is standard equipment.

Electrical system—12-volt system. Delcotron diode-rectified generator with 9-37-ampere rating is standard.

Steering—Recirculating ball-race steering for easiest handling. Ratios: manual, 28.3:1; power, 17:1. Also available is low-ratio steering: manual, 21.6:1; power, 15.6:1.

Camaro SS Sport Coupe with 396-cubic-inch engine and Rally Sport package you can order

goes the way it goes.

Power Trains

Standard Engines—

140-hp Turbo-Thrift 230 Six. Smooth, effortless performance along with a decidedly modest appetite for regular-grade fuel. Single-barrel carburetor, hydraulic valve lifters and single exhaust system. Seven-main-bearing crankshaft.

210-hp Turbo-Fire 327 V8. A perky V8 that will please you with its economy. Its 327-cubic-inch displacement and two-barrel carburetion give it the stamina for all kinds of duty. Compression ratio, 8.75:1, general performance camshaft and hydraulic lifters. A 61-ampere-hour battery and single exhaust. Uses regular-grade fuel.

Extra-Cost Engines—

155-hp Turbo-Thrift 250 Six. Here's a bigger 6-cylinder engine that's excellent for runabout service. Cubic-inch displacement: 250. Single-barrel carburetor, hydraulic valve lifters and single exhaust. Fully counterbalanced seven-main-bearing crankshaft. Uses regular-grade fuel.

275-hp Turbo-Fire 327 V8. Ideally suited to higher performance requirements. Four-barrel carburetor, 327 cubes and a 10.0:1 compression ratio. Single exhaust standard.

295-hp Turbo-Fire 350 V8. One of two Camaro SS engines available. You can judge its credentials by the fact that it powers the SS. A 350-cubic-inch V8, it checks in with a compression ratio of 10.25:1, 4-barrel carburetor, hydraulic valve lifters, dual exhausts and resonators.

325-hp Turbo-Jet 396 V8. Tops in the Camaro stable. Unique feature: "porcupine" cylinder heads that improve engine breathing and combustion. Four-barrel carburetor, 10.25:1 compression ratio, general performance camshaft, hydraulic valve lifters and dual exhausts with resonators.

Standard Transmission—

3-Speed fully synchronized. Standard with all engines except 325-hp V8 (see below). Fully synchronized in all forward gears. Shift lever is column mounted unless floor-mount shift is specified.

Extra-Cost Transmissions—

Special 3-Speed fully synchronized. (Camaro SS only.) Floor-mounted in a snug rubber boot for real shifting fun. Must be specified with 325-hp Turbo-Jet 396 V8 if you order a 3-Speed manual transmission. Offers closer ratios to take advantage of bigger V8 output. (Available with console.)

4-Speed fully synchronized. Floor-mounted and available with all Camaro engines. Available also with console. Tailor-made for the real car buff. Shift pattern is debossed on the control knob. Ratios matched to engine.

Powerglide automatic. Available with all engines except 325-hp V8. Consists of a three-element torque converter with hydraulically controlled two-speed planetary gear set. Selector mounted on steering column if the console is not specified. New "stirrup-type" control with floor console.

Turbo Hydra-Matic. Fully automatic 3-speed transmission available only with the 325-hp Turbo-Jet 396. Combines torque converter and geared drive for a magnificent blend of smoothness and responsiveness. Steering column mounted unless floor-mount is specified, with or without console.

Clutch. Single dry disc diaphragm spring type. Conventional rod and linkage connects suspended pedal to actuating fork. Size and capacity matched to engine choice.

Propeller shaft and rear axle. One-piece balanced propeller shaft, attached at transmission and differential through universal joints. Rear axle ratio matched to power teams.

1968 CAMARO POWER TEAMS

Engines Bore & Stroke	Equipment Compression Ratio	Transmission	Without Air Conditioning*				With Air Conditioning		
			Std.	Econ.	Perform.	Spec.	Std.	Econ.	Perform.
Standard Engines									
140-hp Turbo-Thrift 230 Six 3.875 x 3.25	1-Bbl. Carb. Hyd. Lifters 8.5:1	3-Speed (2.85:1 Low)	3.08:1	2.73:1	3.55:1		3.08:1		3.55:1
		4-Speed (2.85:1 Low)	3.08:1	2.73:1	3.55:1		3.08:1		3.55:1
		Powerglide	2.73:1‡	2.56:1	3.55:1		3.08:1		3.55:1
210-hp Turbo-Fire 327 V8 4.00 x 3.25	2-Bbl. Carb. Hyd. Lifters 8.75:1	3-Speed (2.54:1 Low)	3.08:1	2.73:1	3.55:1		3.08:1		3.55:1
		4-Speed (2.54:1 Low)	3.08:1	2.73:1	3.55:1		3.08:1		3.55:1
		Powerglide	2.73:1‡	2.56:1	3.55:1		3.08:1		3.55:1
Extra-Cost Engines									
155-hp Turbo-Thrift 250 Six 3.875 x 3.53	1-Bbl. Carb. Hyd. Lifters 8.5:1	3-Speed (2.85:1 Low)	3.08:1	2.73:1	3.55:1		3.08:1		3.55:1
		4-Speed (2.85:1 Low)	3.08:1	2.73:1	3.55:1		3.08:1		3.55:1
		Powerglide	2.73:1‡	2.56:1	3.55:1		3.08:1		3.55:1
275-hp Turbo-Fire 327 V8 4.00 x 3.25	4-Bbl. Carb. Hyd. Lifters 10.0:1	3-Speed (2.54:1 Low)	3.08:1	2.73:1	3.55:1		3.08:1		3.55:1
		4-Speed (2.54:1 Low)	3.07:1	2.73:1	3.55:1		3.07:1		3.55:1
		Powerglide	2.73:1‡	2.56:1	3.55:1		3.08:1		3.55:1
295-hp Turbo-Fire 350 V8 4.00 x 3.48	4-Bbl. Carb. Hyd. Lifters 10.25:1	3-Speed (2.54:1 Low)	3.31:1	3.07:1	3.55:1		3.31:1	3.07:1	3.55:1
		Sp. 3-Speed (2.41:1 Low)	3.31:1	3.07:1	3.55:1	3.73:1	3.31:1	3.07:1	3.55:1
		4-Speed (2.52:1 Low)				3.73:1 4.10:1 4.56:1 4.88:1			
		Powerglide	3.07:1	2.73:1	3.31:1	3.55:1 3.73:1	3.07:1	2.73:1	3.31:1
325-hp Turbo-Jet 396 V8 4.094 x 3.76	4-Bbl. Carb. Hyd. Lifters 10.25:1	Sp. 3-Speed (2.41:1 Low)	3.07:1	2.73:1	3.31:1		3.07:1	2.73:1	3.31:1
		4-Speed (2.52:1 Low)	3.07:1	2.73:1	3.31:1		3.07:1	2.73:1	3.31:1
		Turbo Hydra-Matic	2.73:1†	2.56:1	3.07:1		2.73:1‡		3.07:1

*Positraction required for 4.10:1, 4.56:1, 4.88:1, optional for all other ratios. †3.07:1 when Rally Sport is specified. ‡3.08:1 when Rally Sport is specified.

Be Smart • Be Sure • Buy Chevrolet!

Camaro SS Convertible

Litho in U.S.A. D-49491

See our new CUSTOMIZED CAMARO

Come on in and save! All through "Hugger Month" you can be among the first to view the Customized Camaro—latest edition of Chevrolet's exciting personal-size sportster. Featuring four new Camaro colors: Le Mans Blue; Rallye Green; British Green; Corvette Bronze. Plus new mag-spoke wheel covers, new sports striping, whitewall tires, and racy rear deck spoiler—it's a styling first for Camaro you have to see to appreciate. While you're here, you can see and drive all the great "Huggers"... Regular, Rally Sport, Super Sport. There's a personal-size Camaro for every size budget. So drop in during "Hugger Month," and save like never before! See the exciting Customized Camaro and the other sporty '68 Chevrolet models on display at our Chevrolet Sports Department. And bring the whole family down. There's fun for everyone.

Come in now during our "Hugger Month"

CHEVROLET

Ask for me,_____, your Chevrolet Sports Department representative.

I'VE GOT YOUR KIND OF BUY ON A NEW 1968 CHEVROLET

The first of Camaro's sheet metal changes came in 1969. A heavy "eyebrow" crease rose from the front and over the top of the wheel well and then extended along the beltline to the front of the rear wheel well. A matching "eyebrow" went over the rear wheel well and extended to the rear of the quarter panel. Still sitting on a 108-inch wheelbase, the 1969 Camaro was wider and longer, with a more muscular appearance. Non-functional louvers adorned the rear quarter panels, ahead of the wheel wells. The turn signals were round, mounted under the bumper to resemble driving lights.

The Z/28 was shown in the sales brochure for the first time. They called it the strongest Camaro, the one with a mean streak and not everyone's idea of a family sedan. For the second year in a row and twice in three years, the Z/28 took the Trans Am championship, further increasing its popularity.

For 1969, RPO Z-28 included the F-41 handling suspension, twin wide stripes on the hood and trunk lid, a "Z/28" emblem in the grille, "302" emblems on the front fenders and a "Z/28" logo emblazoned on the horn ring. Wheel size was increased to 15x7 inches from the 15x6 inch units previously used, and the tires were now Firestone E70-15 raised-letter series. Power assisted front disc brakes and a four-speed manual transmission were again mandatory options for the Z/28. A cold-air, rear-facing scoop could be ordered to improve engine breathing and four-wheel disc brakes were available as a Regular Production Option. However, due to the high price ($500), only about 200 units were equipped with them, and almost all were on race-prepared cars. Other popular options on the 1969 Z/28 were the rear spoiler, positraction and quicker-ratio steering with power assist.

The 302 engine was now fitted with four-bolt main bearing caps for improved durability. Horsepower was still listed at 290. A variety of manifolds, carburetors and exhaust headers were offered, still delivered in the trunk for after-sale installation.

The more-popular SS Camaro featured a 300 hp 350 V-8 with the 325 hp 396 optional. Again, it could be teamed with a three- or four-speed manual or three-range Turbo Hydramatic transmission. Air conditioning and the convertible body style were additional features available on the SS that could not be had on the Z/28.

The Rally Sport option was available for all Camaros, including the Z/28. For 1969 it included a special grille with concealed headlights on each side. The headlight doors were body color, with three transparent horizontal windows so you could see if the headlights were on behind them. Headlight washers were also included in the RS package; they were optional on all other models. Chrome wheel well moldings and drip rails (on coupes) and bright accents for the simulated louvers on the rear quarter panels were part of the package, as were pinstripes on the "eyebrows" and blacked out rocker panels. On non-SS models, "RS" emblems were placed on the horn ring and between the taillights. Chrome "rally sport" insignia were mounted on the front fenders.

Because an all-new Camaro was being developed for late 1970, production of the 1969 Camaro was extended into the normal 1970 model year. A total of 243,095 Camaros were built during that time, of which 19,014 were Z/28s.

The 1969 Camaro catalogue was again handsome (see pages 32–41). A Chevy sports department catalogue was also issued (see pages 42–45). A Pacesetter Values mailer illustrated the Pace Car Camaro (see page 46, top). The various Camaro-related items used during research on this book appear in the montage below.

WHO NEEDS TO SAY "NEW" OR "BETTER"?

Camaro . . . Chevrolet's incomparable Hugger with the wide-stance grip. Longer, wider, tougher, even quieter for 1969. Decide on a Convertible or Sport Coupe and personalize it from a long list of options and packages. A starter: new Color-Matched resilient bumper that looks like it's part of the car, yet shrugs off nicks and bumps. But put it all together the way *you* want it.

On the cover: Camaro SS Sport Coupe with Rally Sport equipment. Above: Camaro SS Sport Coupe with vinyl roof, Style Trim Group and new Color-Matched bumper you can order...Many extra-cost Options and Custom Features are illustrated or described in this catalog. A convenient listing is on pages 12-13.

3

RALLY SPORT: THIS IS THE SPIRITED WAY TO CHALLENGE A ROAD. JUST ASK THE KID WHO OWNS ONE.

One look and you can see what all the hullaballoo's about. Concealed headlights and a special grille. Rear fender louvers. Headlight washers (that's right, *headlight* washers). You can see why we added a maximum security locking system on the steering column that makes it awfully tough to steal your car. Think we outdid our competition with this one? Good thinking.

Camaro Convertible with Rally Sport equipment.

7

SS: ALL-MUSCLE, ALL-CAR, WITHOUT A TACKY PIECE OF GINGERBREAD ANYWHERE.

Nobody else can come close to Camaro SS. Fat tires. Power disc brakes. Unique hood. Sport striping. Special suspension. Big power. Special 3-Speed transmission with floor shifter. Camaro SS, what the younger generation is coming to because it's about as close as you can come to a pure sports car and still get a back seat and trunk in the deal. We have only one more thing to say: drive it!

Camaro SS Sport Coupe with vinyl roof and Style Trim Group you can order.

The command post.

Camaro, from the rear.   New grille and parking lights.   The Rally Sport's rear trim.

CAMARO

If Camaro looks longer and wider this year, that's because it is. Result: a steadier stance than anything else for this kind of money. There are bucket seats, carpeting, an improved Astro Ventilation system that admits outside air through new rectangular instrument panel vent ports, a wide range of long-lasting Magic-Mirror colors, 25 power team combinations and a new larger tire design. Other refinements you can't see make Camaro so quiet that other sportsters wish they had our secret.

RALLY SPORT

Order a Rally Sport and you'll get features like a unique grille with concealed headlights, bright accented simulated rear fender louvers, fender striping, RS emblems all around, whel opening moldings, black body sill, steering wheel with RS emblem,

INTERIORS

Look. That's the only way to appreciate Camaro's new interiors. You'd think that this is a luxury car, not a lithe and lean sportster. Those tough bucket seats are even more comfortable, and included this year are color-keyed head restraints. The new instrument panel is easy to read and functional (for even more dials to keep track of things, order the Special Instrumentation package). Our interior choices for '69:

STANDARD INTERIOR. All-vinyl bucket seats, matching door and sidewall panels and deep-twist carpeting. Colors: black, ivory-black, blue, red, medium green and dark green. CUSTOM INTERIOR. In addition

Standard Interior.

Extra-cost houndstooth pattern shown in Custom Interior.

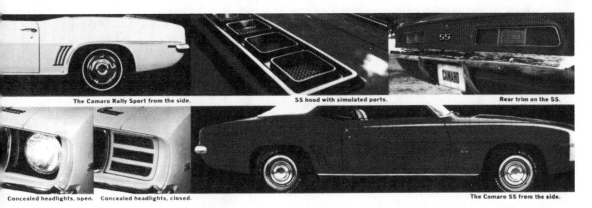

The Camaro Rally Sport from the side.   SS hood with simulated ports.   Rear trim on the SS.

Concealed headlights, open.   Concealed headlights, closed.   The Camaro SS from the side.

SS

chrome-accented tail and parking lights, headlight washers and back-up lights mounted below the rear bumper. Sport Coupe includes roof drip molding. If you want to look like you wrote the book on sportiness, you may specify the SS option—all by itself or with this one.

Camaro SS. The one with a name like the hiss of a snake. Get big power: a 300-hp Turbo-Fire 350 V8. Then, the rest comes easy because it all comes with the car. Special 3-Speed transmission. Sport striping. Special heavily insulated hood.

New white lettered wide-oval tires. Wide wheels. Beefed-up suspension. Power disc brakes. SS identification. Chrome engine accents. Two-spoke steering wheel with SS emblem, bright-accented simulated rear fender louvers. Black body sill. Chrome accents in the right places.

to the features listed, you get bright pedal trim, glove compartment light, the look of wood on instrument panel and steering wheel, special body insulation, luggage compartment mat, built-in armrests, carpeted lower door (Coupe only).

panels and an assist handle on the instrument panel and doors. Colors: black, blue, medium green, dark green, red or a luxury fabric option in black and white houndstooth pattern with black or ivory vinyl.

SPECIAL INTERIOR GROUP. Available as an extra-cost addition to Standard Interior. Includes wood-accented instrument panel and steering wheel, plus a passenger assist handle and bright pedal trim.

Custom Interior you can order.

THIS IS HOW YOU CAN MAKE YOUR CAMARO A SPORTING PROPOSITION.

You can build your Camaro from an economical family car all the way to a spirited sportster with a name to match: Z/28. Read over our power team choices and pick the one that matches your idea of a car. We'll start with our strongest. *Z/28 Camaro.* This is our mean streak. A tough car to match, a hard car to top. Z/28 is a high-performance option package for the Camaro Sport Coupe. Includes a special 290-hp Turbo-Fire 302 V8, quick-ratio steering, special suspension, special white lettered tires, special rally striping, Z/28 emblems and more. Power disc brakes and 4-Speed transmission with Hurst floor-mounted shift are required. Not exactly everyone's idea of a family sedan, so Camaro offers a perfectly matched power team selection that's second to none. Here goes:

POWER TRAINS
Standard Engines
140-hp Turbo-Thrift 230 Six. Get velvet-smooth performance and economy, all in one engine. Single-barrel carburetor, single exhaust system. Seven-main-bearing crankshaft. New quieter operating air cleaner.

210-hp Turbo-Fire 327 V8. This powerplant offers high responsiveness with regular-fuel economy. Two-barrel carburetor, new sturdy construction. Like all '69 Camaro engines, the 327 has a new accessory drive system and a more durable cooling fan design.

Extra-Cost Engines
155-hp Turbo-Thrift 250 Six. Bigger than the standard six, but still provides the economy that you expect. Quieter air cleaner, single-barrel carburetor.

255-hp Turbo-Fire 350 V8. More pep than you would expect for the price, the 350 offers high-performance characteristics on regular-grade fuel. Four-barrel carburetor and sturdier construction.

300-hp Turbo-Fire 350 V8. For Camaro SS only. That, right there, tells you a lot. A performance standout all the way. Four-barrel carburetor, dual exhausts, new stronger construction, tougher cylinder blocks, improved fuel handling system and extra-firm four-bolt main bearing cap attachment.

325 hp Turbo-Jet 396 V8. Camaro's "boss" engine. Unique "porcupine" cylinder heads for maximum engine breathing and combustion. Four-barrel carburetor and dual exhausts.

Standard Transmission
3-Speed fully synchronized. Comes with all six-cylinder and standard V8 engines. Shift lever is column-mounted unless floor-mount is specified.

Extra-Cost Transmissions
Special 3-Speed fully synchronized. Available with 255-hp 350 V8 and Camaro SS engines only. A more durable design for '69. Floor-mounted shift in a snug rubber boot. Closer ratios than the Standard Unit to utilize bigger V8 output. Available with console.

4-Speed fully synchronized. Can be had with all Camaro engines. This sporty transmission with Hurst floor shift is ratio-matched to your engine. Shift pattern is debossed on control knob. Available with console.

Torque-Drive. Available only on six-cylinder engines. A new no-clutch approach to driving. Torque-Drive eliminates the clutch pedal and offers excellent fuel economy.

Powerglide. This fully automatic transmission offers smooth, effortless performance. Selector is mounted on steering column if console is not specified. "Stirrup-type" control comes with floor console.

Turbo Hydra-Matic. Automatic 3-speed shifting with torque converter and geared drive for extra smoothness and responsiveness. Selector-mounted on column or floor-mounted with console. Can be used as a fully automatic transmission or, if you like, shift it manually through the gears.

CHASSIS AND MECHANICAL FEATURES

Body by Fisher. This quality trademark assures you Camaro is strong and well built. Rugged body components are used throughout. Camaro's unitized all-welded steel body with a separate rubber-mounted front frame provides support, strength and silence. Rust? We've done our best to prevent it with galvanized body members, four inner fenders and flush-and-dry rocker panels.

Handling and suspension. Camaro sits on a 108-inch wheelbase with a 59.6-inch front tread. Camaro's wide stance design gives you hard-to-equal cornering and handling. New computer-selected front and rear springs provide more precise trim and height. Independent coil spring front suspension and Mono-Plate single-leaf rear springs (standard V8 and six-cylinder engines) or multi-leaf rear springs (optional V8s) give you road-hugging control.

Brakes. Safety-Master self-adjusting brakes include finned front brake drums and quieter linings. Brakes have dual master cylinder with instrument panel warning light.

What else makes Camaro a standout?
Electrical system: Delcotron diode-rectified generator with 37-ampere rating.
Exhaust system: Corrosion-resistant for long life.
Anti-interference ignition system: New spark plugs and ignition wiring help minimize radio signal interference.
Steering: Recirculating ball-race steering. Overall ratios: Manual, 27.3:1; power, 15.5:1 to 11.8:1. Quick-ratio steering available: manual, 21.4:1; power, 14.3:1 to 10.9:1.

COLORS

Choose from a wide range of Camaro Magic-Mirror finishes. New two-tone combinations are available on the Sport Coupe. Convertible top can be had in black or white. Vinyl roof cover comes in black, parchment, midnight green, dark blue or dark brown. Our colors include:
☐ Dover White ☐ Glacier Blue ☐ Le Mans Blue ☐ Olympic Gold ☐ Azure Turquoise ☐ Frost Green ☐ Cortez Silver ☐ Garnet Red ☐ Fathom Green ☐ Hugger Orange ☐ Daytona Yellow ☐ Rallye Green ☐ Dusk Blue ☐ Burnished Brown ☐ Burgundy

1969 STANDARD SAFETY FEATURES

In 1969 all Camaros feature an impressive array of safety, anti-theft and convenience equipment, more notable among these are:
☐ Energy absorbing steering column ☐ Seat belts with pushbutton buckles for *all* passenger positions ☐ Shoulder belts with pushbutton buckles and special storage convenience provision for driver and right front passenger (except convertibles) ☐ Two front seat head restraints ☐ Passenger guard door locks—with forward mounted lock buttons ☐ Four-way hazard warning flasher ☐ Dual master cylinder brake system with warning light and corrosion resistant brake lines ☐ Folding seat back latches ☐ Dual speed windshield wipers and washers ☐ Dual action safety hood latch ☐ Outside rear view mirror ☐ Backup lights ☐ Side marker lights and parking lamps that illuminate with headlamps ☐ Energy absorbing instrument panel ☐ Padded sun visors ☐ Reduced glare instrument panel top, inside windshield moldings, horn buttons, steering wheel hub, and windshield wiper arms and blades ☐ Wide inside day-night mirror with deflecting base ☐ Lane change feature in direction signal control ☐ Safety arm rests ☐ Thick laminate windshield ☐ Soft, low-profile window control knobs, coat hooks, dome lamp ☐ Padded front seat back tops ☐ Smooth contoured door and window regulator handles ☐ Anti-theft ignition key warning buzzer ☐ Anti-theft ignition, steering and transmission lock ☐ Starter safety switch on all transmissions ☐ Tire safety rim ☐ Safety door latches and hinges ☐ Uniform shift quadrant

1969 CAMARO POWER TEAMS					
			REAR AXLE RATIO (:1)*		
				Optional	
ENGINES	TRANSMISSIONS	Std.	Econ.	Perf.	Spcl.
Standard Engines					
140-hp Turbo-Thrift 230 Six	3-Speed (2.85:1 Low)	3.08	2.73	3.36	
	4-Speed (2.85:1 Low)				
	Torque-Drive	2.73			
	Powerglide				
	Turbo Hydra-Matic	2.73	2.56	3.08	3.36
210-hp Turbo-Fire 327 V8	3-Speed (2.54:1 Low)	3.08	2.73	3.36	
	4-Speed (2.54:1 Low)				
	Powerglide				
	Turbo Hydra-Matic	2.73	2.56		3.36
Extra-Cost Engines					
155-hp Turbo-Thrift 250 Six	3-Speed (2.85:1 Low)	3.08	2.73	3.36	
	4-Speed (2.85:1 Low)				
	Torque-Drive	2.73			
	Powerglide				
	Turbo Hydra-Matic	2.73	2.56	3.08	3.36
255-hp Turbo-Fire 350 V8	Special 3-Speed (2.42:1 Low)	3.31	3.07	3.55	3.73
	4-Speed (2.52:1 Low)				3.73 4.10
	Powerglide				
	Turbo Hydra-Matic	3.08	2.73	3.36	3.55
300-hp Turbo-Fire 350 V8	Special 3-Speed (2.42:1 Low)				3.73
	4-Speed (2.52:1 Low)	3.31	3.07	3.55	3.73 4.10
	Powerglide				
	Turbo Hydra-Matic	3.08	2.73	3.36	3.55
325-hp Turbo-Jet 396 V8	Special 3-Speed (2.42:1 Low)	3.07	2.73	3.31	
	4-Speed (2.52:1 Low)				
	Turbo Hydra-Matic	3.07	2.73		2.56

Positraction required for 3.73, 4.10; optional for all others. For ratios that apply to models with air conditioning consult your dealer.

CAMARO SS/RS

CAMARO After Corvette what do you say...besides Camaro?

And to come this close to Corvette we picked the best sports-car brains around (our own).

APPEARANCE FEATURES

EXTERIOR—To follow in Corvette's footsteps, you've got to look as well as act the part. Flared fender lines help show off "The Hugger." V-shaped grille sweeps in on each side to shrouded headlights. (RS versions hide headlights completely.) Now check other particulars.

SS (RPO Z27):
Special hood with simulated ports. A tapered stripe along the side. Black body sill; black rear panel with 396 V8. Special steering wheel, white-lettered tires on 7"-wide rims and special suspension. Power disc brakes and special 3-Speed. SS includes a 300-hp Turbo-Fire 350 V8. A 325-hp Turbo-Jet 396 can be ordered (RPO L35). SS can be specified along with RS.

RS (RALLY SPORT) (RPO Z22):
Special grille with panels to hide headlights when not in use. And nozzles are now included that shoot a stream of washing fluid to rid headlights of dirt. Bright wheel opening moldings. Back-up lights below the bumper. RS can be ordered along with SS ("RS" identification replaced by "SS").

Z/28 (RPO Z28):
Makes a full blown 4-place sports car. You get a special 302 cubic-incher topped with aluminum intake manifold, huge 4-barrel carburetor, dual throaty-tone exhausts. Stiffer suspension, 15" wheels. Positive Hurst shift linkage on the 4-Speed. Power disc brakes included. Broad stripes running over the hood and rear deck.

Style Trim Group (RPO Z21): Fender striping; bright fender opening moldings; black body sill.

Front accent striping (RPO DX1): Wide striping across nose and down center of hood.

CAMARO POWER TEAMS

Fender striping (RPO D96): Striping follows front of wheel opening contours and extends along body. Included with RPO Z21 and RS.

Sport striping (RPO D90): Wide striping from front fenders rearward into door. (Included with SS.)

Color-Matched resilient front bumper (RPO VE3): Steel reinforced plastic in body color. Surface "gives" and re-forms itself to hide minor bumps and scrapes.

INTERIOR—Bucket seats in front. Better cockpit air circulation with Astro Ventilation's rectangular vent-ports on instrument panel.

With Camaro's new locking system, ignition, steering wheel and shift lever are all locked. Head restraints on front seats. Carpeting. Six standard all-vinyl interiors including black, ivory/black, blue, red, medium green and midnight green.

Custom Interior (RPO Z87): Available in four all-vinyl interiors, plus a houndstooth pattern-cloth seat trim with either a black or ivory trim. Door panels have assist grip and built-in armrests; carpet at the lower edge. Bright pedal trim and steering wheel with wood-grain accents. Glove compartment light, special insulation and luggage compartment mat.

Special Interior Group (RPO Z23): Bright pedal trim and steering wheel with wood-grain accents.

MECHANICAL FEATURES

ENGINES—One V8 for SS is a 300-hp Turbo-Fire 350; another V8 is a 325-hp Turbo-Jet 396. For the Z/28, there's the brilliant 302-cu.-in. V8 with the throaty rumble out the exhaust. "Inboard balancing" locates all accessories closer to the engine for quieter, more durable operation. 300-hp V8 has finned, cast-aluminum rocker covers. Z/28 Camaro engine has solid valve lifters and special cam.

ENGINE	TRANSMISSION	REAR AXLE RATIO (:1)*			
		Std.	Optional		
			Econ.	Perf.	Spcl.
Turbo-Fire 350 350-Cu.-In. V8 300 HP @ 4800 4-bbl. carb. 10.25:1 C.R. Premium fuel	Special 3-Speed (2.42:1 Low)				3.73
	4-Speed (2.52:1 Low)	3.31	3.07	3.55	3.73 4.10
	Powerglide				
	Turbo Hydra-Matic	3.08	2.73	3.36	3.55
Turbo-Jet 396 396-Cu.-In. V8 325 HP @ 4800 4-bbl. carb. 10.25:1 C.R. Premium fuel RPO L35	Special 3-Speed (2.42:1 Low)	3.07	2.73	3.31	
	4-Speed (2.52:1 Low)				
	Turbo Hydra-Matic				2.56
Turbo-Fire 302 302-Cu.-In. V8 290 HP @ 5800 4-bbl. carb. 11.0:1 C.R. Premium fuel RPO Z/28 (Spt. Cpe. only)	4-Speed (2.52:1 Low)	3.73	3.55	4.10	
	4-Speed (2.20:1 Low)				3.07 3.31
	Special 4-Speed (2.20:1 Low)				

*Without Air Conditioning. Positraction required for 3.73 (except Z/28), 4.10; optional for all others.

TRANSMISSIONS—Column-mounted lever with standard 3-Speed (floor-mounted available) and automatics. Lever goes in console, if so equipped. A starter safety switch prevents accidental in-gear starts. *Special 3-Speed*—a heavy-duty floor version standard with SS. *4-Speed*—order with any engine and a Hurst floor shifter is standard. (4-Speed is required with Z/28 Camaro.) *Powerglide*—2-speed fully automatic. *Turbo Hydra-Matic*—a 3-speed fully automatic; can be shifted manually "through the gears" if desired with the 1—2—3 selector positions.

CHASSIS-SUSPENSION-REAR AXLE—Unitized all-welded steel body construction with separate front frame section. Independent coil spring front suspension; stabilizer bar. Multi-leaf rear springs. F70 x 14 white lettered tires on SS. E70 x 15 on Z/28. Wider 7″ wheel rims with SS and Z/28. Two power disc brake options: 1) front discs with single-piston caliper and drum-type rear (included with SS and Z/28); 2) 4-wheel disc brakes with four-piston calipers, as in Corvette (includes 15″ wheels). New variable-ratio power steering available; gives faster turning in tight maneuvering; still retains positive "feel."

POPULAR EXTRA-COST OPTIONS ☐ Air spoiler equipment ☐ Headlight washers (included with RS equipment) ☐ Stereo tape system ☐ AM-FM radio ☐ Air conditioning with improved cooling efficiency ☐ Sports console ☐ Tachometer ☐ Special instrumentation ☐ Comfortilt steering wheel ☐ Wheel covers, including simulated wire, mag-spoke, mag-style or trim rings ☐ Sport wheels for SS. ☐ Rally wheels ☐ Space saver spare tire ☐ Power steering ☐ Power windows ☐ Positraction ☐ Rear deck luggage carrier ☐ Vinyl roof cover ☐ Engine-block heater.

CAMARO RS CONVERTIBLE

CAMARO SS GRILLE AND HOOD

AIR SPOILER EQUIPMENT WITH Z/28 STRIPING

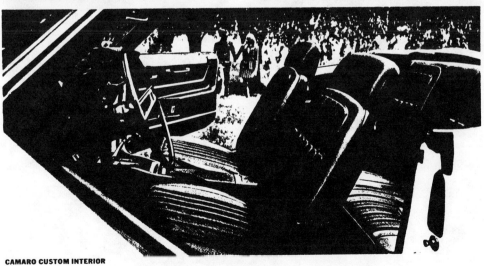

CAMARO CUSTOM INTERIOR

1970

February 26, 1970, marked the dawn of a new era; an all-new fastback Camaro debuted. The body style was called a classic by many automotive experts; some hailed it as one of the most beautiful designs ever. And, by American standards, it achieved near immortality; the basic body shape remained unchanged for more than a decade.

Gone was the convertible. The only configuration available was the fastback. Although still sitting on a 108-inch wheelbase, the new Camaro didn't share a single body panel with its predecessor. The product lineup remained the same, though: base, Rally Sport, Super Sport and Z/28. But the slash was dropped from the Z/28 designation; now it was just Z28.

The Z28 concept changed as well. With the SCCA rule change allowing destroking to comply with displacement requirements, the 302 engine was discontinued in favor of the 350. The engine used was basically the same one used in the Corvette. Using solid lifters, a hot cam, extruded aluminum pistons, extra large valves and a Holley 780 cfm four-barrel carburetor, the Z28 engine was the highest rated engine in the Camaro lineup, putting out a healthy 360 hp — 10 more than the 396 engine available in the SS package.

Along with the new 350 engine, the Z28 option included the F-41 handling suspension, quick-ratio steering, a larger radiator, the familiar twin wide stripes on the hood and trunk and F60-15 raised-letter fiberglass-belted tires mounted on 15x7 inch rims. For the first time, a spoiler (mounted on the trunk lip) was included in the package.

Another first for the Z28 that year was the availability of an automatic transmission; the three-range Turbo Hydramatic could be ordered instead of the four-speed manual with Hurst linkage. As in previous years, the Z28 could be ordered in base or Rally Sport versions.

The Rally Sport package had a very distinctive look to it. Instead of a full front bumper, bumperettes flanked a blacked-out floating grille circled by a body-colored Endura surround. A black strip of the same material was placed vertically in the center to protect the grille from small accidents. The parking/turn signals were shifted from below the front bumper to round housings in the catwalks between the grille and headlights. This gave the Camaro a very dramatic and European look. For a cleaner line, the wipers disappeared below the rear hood lip. An "RS" emblem was mounted in the center of the steering wheel and "RALLY SPORT" emblems were mounted on each front fender. The RS package was available on base, SS and Z28 models.

The engines offered on the SS Camaros were not as strong as the Z28's 360 hp. The standard 350 was only rated at 300 hp; the big-block 396 was listed at only 350. With the demise of the convertible and availability of an automatic in the Z28, the only advantage the SS enjoyed was being able to order air conditioning, a luxury still not offered on Z28s.

Many experts hailed the 1970 Z28 as the greatest Z of all, with the strongest engine, the best looks (unmarred by federal regulations) and terrific handling. Unfortunately, due to the shortened production year, only 8,733 of a total production of 124,889 Camaros were Z28s.

The 1970 Camaro catalogue was still handsome (see pages 48-53). A pair of Chevy sports department mailers were also issued (see pages 54-55). A Chevy salesman's ponycar comparisons folder is reproduced on pages 56-58. The various Camaro-related items used during research on this book appear in the montage below.

Before you go diving right into this page, hold on just one second. Flip the right page out.

There. Now, take a good long look at the Camaro Rally Sport.

Up front there's a blacked-out grille. It looks so big and mouthy, that it makes Camaro's wide stance seem even wider.

And it's surrounded with a resilient, color-matched frame that acts as a bumper. Then, there's a vertical bar down the middle of the grille. It's resilient, too (a special kind of rubber). So, if somebody gives you a klunk, there are no bruises. And no hurt feelings.

But that's not all the bumper you get. There's a split-bumper that wraps clear around to both sides of the front end.

And see those lights? One's a rally-styled parking light. The other, Camaro's high-intensity

RS

headlight. They set the Rally Sport apart from other cars. Even in the dark. (You can see it on the back page.)

There are windshield wipers that tuck out of sight. Flared wheel openings like you see on expensive sports cars. Bucket seats. And bright styling accents that give it looks on top of looks.

And on the steering wheel, there's a big, bright RS emblem so you always know you've got something special.

Just watch. When you pull up in this one, you'll get a lot more than admiring glances.

(Now, flip the right-hand page back, and this one out.)

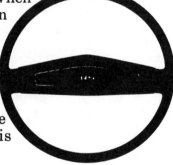

SS Now that you've seen both the RS and SS, here comes the big decision.

Which one you want more.

Go back. Take another look at both.

...... are you with us again?

Good. Now we'll fill you in on the SS. (Might help you make up your mind which one you like better.)

This is the car for you if you really look forward to getting behind the wheel. Even if it's just to visit somebody down the street.

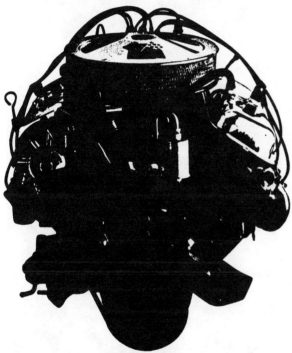

The standard engine you get is a 300-horse 350-cubic-inch V8 that inhales through 4-barrel carb and exhales through dual exhausts. If you want still more, you can order the 350-horse 396-cubic-inch V8. When you order this big one you get a special suspension with a rear stabilizer bar. Both engines require 4-speed or Turbo Hydra-matic. That way you've got all the horses in the palm of your hand.

With the SS you also get hood insulation, and black-painted grille and back panel. The rubber is white-lettered F70x14 on 7"-wide wheels. Front disc brakes are standard on the SS, too. But with this package they're power assisted.

And in case you couldn't find the windshield wipers, relax. They're the Hide-A-Way kind.

We even added something for the benefit of other cars. Distinctive SS identification. That way they'll always know what they're up against.

But the best thing is, you don't have to be rich to make the scene.

When you go driving in this one, have the neighbors take your mail.

You might be gone for a while.

Camaro Sport Coupe with Z28 package.

Z28

This is the Camaro Z28. It's not for everybody.

We recommend it for the guy who always wanted a performance car that he could drive to work.

Let's start with the engine. It's a special 360-horse Turbo-Fire 350 V8. And there's a lot that's special about it. Like the cam. The mechanical lifters. The big 4-barrel carb. Everything spells performance.

But there's more to it than that.

You also get extruded aluminum pistons. Extra-large intake and exhaust valves. And a thermo-modulated fan that cuts in when the engine needs more cool.

Same thing with the transmission. Order 4-speed with a Hurst linkage. Gives you short crisp throws. If you want to go the automatic route, you can order the Turbo Hydra-matic. It's a three-range setup that shifts itself or lets you take over.

The suspension?

Ditto. There are higher rate springs with matching shocks at all four wheels. A stabilizer bar in the rear as well as the front. Combine all that with the Z28's quick-ratio steering and you'll move through corners flat and precise.

Then, there are other performance telltales. Special wheels with F60x15 white-lettered tires. Heavy-duty radiator. Special Z28 striping. And a rear-deck air spoiler.

Now, that's what we call a healthy car.

One more thing. When you come to see the "Z," make sure you've got your driving gloves.

If that isn't enough to get your adrenalin flowing, there's a Corvette catalog not too far away.

Our things for yours.

Camaro Options.
Let's suppose somebody on the next block has a new Camaro, too. That's nice, but no two Camaros have to be exactly alike. Here's how you can do it up your way.

Deluxe Bumpers
Here's something that looks as good as it works. A thick rubber strip is added to the entire length of the front and rear bumpers. They take the sting out of hard knocks.

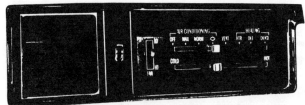

Four-Season Air Conditioning
It's a nice thing to have when the heat's on outside. Adjust the controls, roll up the windows and enjoy the cool (V8 models only).

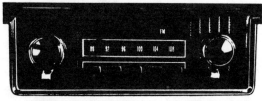

AM/FM Radio
The Camaro itself is entertaining enough. But some good sounds can make it better yet. And see those little lines in the windshield? That's the antenna. That's right, the antenna.

Special Instrumentation
Forget the tack-on-tach. Ours is on the instrument panel, along with a temperature gauge and an ammeter. There's even a clock to show you what good times you're making.

Center Console
The action is right here whether you order manual or automatic transmissions. You get it with simulated wood, storage compartment and courtesy light.

Custom Interior
With such a great looking outside, why not order an extra special inside?

You can take your choice of all-vinyl buckets in five colors (black, bright blue, dark green, saddle or sandalwood). Or you can specify a luxury fabric in any of four colors (black, black/bright blue, black/dark green, or black/white).

You also get wood-grain accents on instrument cluster panel, door trim panels and steering wheel, extra body insulation, luggage compartment mat and more. Now, that's what we call plush.

Sport Mirrors

Expensive sports cars have streamlined mirrors like this. So does Camaro. They're color matched and come with remote control on the driver's side.

Your Chevy dealer has a complete list of Options and Custom Features.

Standard Safety Features

Occupant Protection

Seat belts with pushbutton buckles for all passenger positions. Shoulder belts with pushbutton buckles—driver and right front passenger. Two front-seat head restraints. Energy-absorbing steering column. Passenger-guard door locks with forward mounted lock buttons. Safety door latches and hinges. Folding seat back latches. Energy-absorbing instrument panel and front seat back tops. Thick-laminate windshield. Padded sun visors. Safety armrests. Safety steering wheel. Side-guard door beam. Cargo-guard luggage compartment. Double panel roof structure with integral headers.

Accident Prevention

Side marker lights and reflectors. Parking lights that illuminate with headlights. Four-way hazard warning flasher. Backup lights. Lane-change feature in directional signal control. Windshield defroster, washer and dual speed wipers. Wide-view inside day-night mirror (vinyl-edged, shatter-resistant glass). Outside rearview mirror. Bias belted ply tires with tire tread wear indicators. Dual master cylinder brake system with warning light. Starter safety switch. Dual-action safety hood latches.

Anti-theft

Anti-theft ignition key warning buzzer. Anti-theft steering column lock. Anti-theft door lock buttons.

CAMARO POWER TEAMS						
ENGINES	TRANSMISSIONS	REAR AXLE RATIOS	COMPRESSION RATIO	TORQUE	CARBURETION	REQUIRED FUEL
STANDARD ENGINES						
155-hp Turbo Thrift 250 Six	3-Speed	3.08	8.5:1	235 lb-ft. @ 1600 rpm	Single barrel	Regular
	Powerglide	2.73				
200-hp Turbo-Fire 307 V8	3-Speed	3.08	9.0:1	300 lb-ft. @ 2400 rpm	Two barrel	Regular
	Powerglide	2.73				
	Turbo Hydra-matic	2.73				
EXTRA-COST ENGINES						
250-hp Turbo-Fire 350	4-Speed	3.36	9.0:1	345 lb-ft. @ 2800 rpm	Two barrel	Regular
	Turbo Hydra-matic	2.73				
300-hp Turbo-Fire 350 V8 (SS only)	4-Speed	3.31	10.25:1	380 lb-ft. @ 3200 rpm	Four barrel	Premium
	Turbo Hydra-matic	3.07				
360-hp Turbo-Fire 350 V8 (Z28 only)	4-Speed	3.73 or Special Option 4.10	11.00:1	380 lb-ft. @ 4500 rpm	Four barrel	Premium
	Turbo Hydra-matic					
350-hp Turbo-Jet 396 V8 (SS only)	4-Speed	3.31	10.25:1	415 lb-ft. @ 3400 rpm	Four barrel	Premium
	Turbo Hydra-matic					

New Camaro with Rally Sport Package.

New Corvette

They're revving and waiting for you.

Hot off the assembly line! New Camaro. New Corvette. They're not for everyone. They weren't built to be. Camaro and Corvette are for those who really dig driving.

Take Camaro. It comes on strong with a whole new look. Outside, there's less chrome, more class. Inside, there's a wraparound dash, bucket seats up front and bucket cushions in the rear. Front disc brakes come standard. So does an improved road-grabbing suspension. Under the hood: up to 360 horses in the Z28 version.

What's new about Corvette, America's only true production-built sports car? Styling's been refined, but the aerodynamic look that sets Corvette apart, is still there. There's a new Custom Interior available that includes leather seat trim, plush cut-pile carpeting, and special wood-like door trim. How does all this move? Up to 390 horses strong, with a new 454 V8 you can order. That's how!

New Camaro. New Corvette. If you get a charge out of driving, these are the babies for you. See them soon at our Sports Department.

_____
(SALESMAN'S NAME)

Catch the action now at our Sports Department.

Camaro, Chevelle SS, Monte Carlo SS, Nova SS and Corvette.
From our Sports Department.

We've got the largest selection of sports models. We can make a big improvement in the way you drive. Just name the way you want to go. We've got it. From the out and out luxury of the Monte Carlo SS to Corvette, the favorite American sports car.

So if you think you'd like to try the sportin' life, see us first.

We're pros, too. Everybody has something they do best. We're No. 1 at selling cars and we're professionals at saving you money. Right now we've got a bag full of deals and a lot full of cars. So drop by. We'll be happy to give you a money-saving driving lesson.

Chevelle SS

Camaro RS

'70 CAMARO WINS TOP HONORS

OVER MUSTANG, CHALLENGER
AND BARRACUDA

- ■ EXTERIOR STYLING
- ■ INTERIOR STYLING
- ■ MECHANICAL FEATURES
  - ● BRAKING
  - ● HANDLING
  - ● CONSTRUCTION

YOU HAVE SOMETHING BETTER
The NEW CAMARO

CHECK THE SCORE YOURSELF!!!

CHECKPOINT	CAMARO	MUSTANG	CHALLENGER	BARRACUDA
BODY STYLES:	1	3	3	2
PERFORMANCE:				
Engines	7	6	9	9
base six	250 CID	200 CID	225 CID	225 CID
	155 HP	120 HP	145 HP	145 HP
largest V8	396 CID	426 CID	440 CID	440 CID
	375 HP	335 HP	390 HP	390 HP
Transmissions	4	3	3	3
Power Teams	14	15	18	21

YOUR SELLING ADVANTAGE

One-of-a-kind Camaro delivers the most popular appearance trends in the sporty car field, takes on a whole new "feel" with style trim, Z/28, "SS", Rally Sport, "RS-SS" and "RS"-Z/28 model options.

Camaro has one more engine than Mustang—largest base six and one more transmission than Mustang, Challenger and Barracuda. Those 14 power teams offer plenty of versatility.

CHECKPOINT	CAMARO 2-Dr. Fastback	MUSTANG 2-Dr. Hardtop	CHALLENGER 2-Dr. Hardtop	BARRACUDA 2-Dr. Hardtop
COMPARATIVE EXTERIOR DIMENSIONS:				
Height	50.5"	51.5"	50.9"	50.9"
Width	74.4"	71.7"	76.1"	74.7"
Length	188.0"	187.4"	191.3"	186.7"
Tread: Front	61.3"	58.5"	59.7"	60.2"
Rear	60.0"	58.5"	60.7"	58.3"
Wheelbase	108.0"	108.0"	110.0"	108.0"
Tire Size	E78 x 14"	E78 x 14"	E78 x 14"	E78 x 14"
Total Exposed Glass Area (sq. in.)	3,326	2,897	3,206	3,164

YOUR SELLING ADVANTAGE

Camaro's longer than last year, lower than all competition. Passenger compartment is moved three inches rearward for a better front-to-rear weight ratio, includes more total exposed glass area, with wider combined wheel tread dimensions. New Camaro's lean, clean body lines put Camaro years ahead of competition.

Exclusively Camaro:
- Double Panel Roof
- Hood Stop Pins
- Steel Inner Front Fenders
- Flush-and-Dry Rocker Panels
- Power Beam Headlamps

CHECKPOINT	CAMARO 2-Dr. Fastback	MUSTANG 2-Dr. Hardtop	CHALLENGER 2-Dr. Hardtop	BARRACUDA 2-Dr. Hardtop
COMPARATIVE INTERIOR DIMENSIONS:				
Front Compartment				
Effective Headroom	37.4"	37.3"	37.4"	37.4"
Maximum Legroom	43.8"	40.0"	42.3"	42.3"
Shoulder Room	56.7"	56.0"	58.1"	57.5"
Hip Room	57.7"	55.6"	56.9"	57.1"
Rear Compartment				
Effective Headroom	36.1"	35.7"	35.6"	35.7"
Minimum Legroom	29.6"	28.8"	30.9"	28.9"
Shoulder Room	54.4"	54.7"	56.6"	55.3"
Hip Room	47.3"	51.3"	55.0"	52.0"
Total Rear-Compartment Room	23.6"	21.3"	22.1"	20.1"
Luggage Compartment				
Total Luggage Compartment Area	7.3 Cu. ft.	9.2 Cu. ft.	5.9 Cu. ft.	5.9 Cu. ft.

YOUR SELLING ADVANTAGE

Camaro combines roominess with an "in-and-under" sports car seating that performance enthusiasts expect. Front seats rake back; rear seat cushions have "bucket-seat" contours. Camaro has full-depth-foam front seat back and front and rear seat cushions against competition's less expensive, less comfortable foam sheet and cotton-padded seats.

None of the competition matches Camaro's easy-to-read, easy-to-reach cockpit-type instrument panel. And "Side Guard" door beams insure maximum occupant protection.

Exclusively Camaro:
- Air-Gap Windshield Pillars
- Cargo-Guard Barrier
- Wider Doors

CHECKPOINT	CAMARO 2-Dr. Fastback	MUSTANG 2-Dr. Hardtop	CHALLENGER 2-Dr. Hardtop	BARRACUDA 2-Dr. Hardtop
COMPARATIVE WHEELS AND BRAKES:				
Wheel Rim Dia.	14" x 6"	14" x 6"	14 x 5"	14" x 5"
Optional Rim Dia.	14" x 7"**	14" x 7"	14" x 5.5"	14" x 5.5"
Front Brake Type				
Standard	disc	drum	drum	drum
Optional	—	disc	disc	disc
Rear Brake Type				
Standard	drum	drum	drum	drum
Linings	bonded	riveted	riveted	riveted
Brake Swept Area (sq. in.)	332.4	251.2	314.2	314.2

Manual Front Disc Brakes . . . Standard

New Camaro is equipped with standard manual front disc brakes which give straight-ahead braking response with greater fade resistance and cooler operation. Power assist is available optionally. And Camaro's front wheel hub and disc brake rotor are combined into a new single unit, integral casting design.

Every effort has been made to provide accurate, current and correct data. However, the Chevrolet Motor Division does not assume responsibility for inaccuracies or errors.

*14 x 7 wheels included in Camaro "SS" package; 15 x 7 wheels included in Camaro Z/28 package.

Produced by: Chevrolet New Car Merchandising Department

CHECKPOINT	CAMARO 2-Dr. Fastback	MUSTANG 2-Dr. Hardtop	CHALLENGER 2-Dr. Hardtop	BARRACUDA 2-Dr. Hardtop
COMPARATIVE STEERING AND SUSPENSION DATA:				
Turning Diameters Curb-to-Curb	38.86	37.8	39.32	38.77
Front Suspension	Full coil	Full coil	Torsion bar	Torsion bar
Rear Suspension	Multiple leaf sprgs	Multiple leaf sprgs	Longitudinal leaf	Longitudinal leaf
Provision for car leveling	Stab. Bar	Stab. Bar	Man. adj. anch. bolt	Man. adj. anch. bolt

• CAMARO'S SUSPENSION SECRET . . .

Up front, a redesigned suspension system with a wider front tread gives the ideal design for Camaro's weight and size. Basic design uses the ''A''-shaped upper and lower control arms—but the bushing span has been widened considerably. The upper arm is straighter, the ball-joint span wider and the lower ball-joint larger. Staggered shock absorbers have new valving for stiffer action, to reduce body roll and axle windup. Lateral shake and body roll are reduced with new rear-spring bushings.

Camaro's separate front frame spells a big difference on the open road. The frame itself is stronger, uses fewer individual pieces. Side rails are larger box sections and a single, larger front cross member lends extra beef.

The total payoff: exceptional wheel control and increased durability.

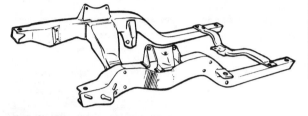

COMPARATIVE PRICES:

	Base Six	Base V8
CAMARO		
2-Door ''Fastback'' Sports Coupe	$2749	$2839
• Camaro ''RS'' Rally Sport	——	$3008
• Camaro ''SS'' Super Sport	——	$3129
• Camaro Z/28	——	$3412
• Camaro ''RS''-Z/28	——	$3580
MUSTANG		
2-Door Hardtop	$2721	$2822
2-Door Fastback	$2771	$2872
Grande 2-Door Hardtop	$2926	$3028
Mach I 2-Door Fastback	——	$3271
Boss 302 2-Door Fastback	——	$3720
Convertible	$3025	$3126
CHALLENGER		
2-Door Hardtop	$2851	$2953
2-Door Hardtop Special Edition	$3083	$3185
Convertible	$3120	$3222
• R/T 2-Door Hardtop	——	$3266
• R/T 2-Door Hardtop Special Edition	——	$3498
• R/T Convertible	——	$3535
BARRACUDA		
2-Door Hardtop	$2764	$2865
Convertible	$3034	$3135
Gran Coupe 2-Door Hardtop	$2934	$3035
Gran Coupe Convertible	$3160	$3260
• ''Cuda'' 2-Door Hardtop	——	$3164
• ''Cuda'' Convertible	——	$3433

Manufacturer's Suggested Retail Prices

CAMARO MONEY BUYS MORE

CHECKPOINT	CAMARO 2-Dr. Fastback	MUSTANG 2-Dr. Hardtop	CHALLENGER 2-Dr. Hardtop	BARRACUDA 2-Dr. Hardtop
COMPARATIVE CONSTRUCTION FEATURES:				
Partial Front Frame	Yes	No	No	No
Double Panel Roof	Yes	No	No	No
Hood Stop Pins	Yes	No	No	No
Air-Gap Windshield Pillars	Yes	No	No	No
Cargo-Guard Luggage Barrier	Yes	No	No	No
''Side Guard'' Door Beams	Yes	No	Yes	Yes
Steel Inner Fenders	Yes	No	No	No
Flush-and-Dry Rocker Panels	Yes	No	No	No

EXCLUSIVELY CAMARO

Partial Front Frame:
Exclusive partial front frame delivers greater shock resistance, more comfort than competition's bolted-together ''unibody'' construction.
New Camaro takes a wide lead in quietness, roadability and rattle-free dependability.

Double Steel Panel Roof:
Two steel panels provide stronger structure above, improved sound absorption. Inner panel is used to form strong box sections for integral windshield header, side rails and rear header.

Hood Stop Pins:
Added to hood hinges to limit rearward movement in the event of front impact.

Air-Gap Windshield Pillars, Cargo-Guard Luggage Barrier,''Side Guard''Door Beams:
Added construction / safety features for passenger protection. (Mustang does not have comparable door guard beams.)

New Power Beam Headlamps:
Camaro's new single headlamp system provides 14 percent brighter illumination than conventional single lamp systems in low beam, seven percent brighter illumination in high beam. Power beam headlamps have more brilliance and a greater effective area in low beam, project light a greater distance with less glare in high beam operation.

Steel Inner Fenders, Galvanized Flush-and-Dry Rocker Panels:
Both stop corrosive elements to help keep new Camaro looking young longer. Steel inner fenders help ''quiet'' the ride, too!

With the 1970 Camaro only a half year old, there was no point in making any cosmetic changes for 1971, so Chevrolet didn't. The grille, taillights and emblems all remained the same. A small change was made in mid-year, perhaps in an economy move; the low-back front seats were replaced by high back versions borrowed from the Vega.

Under the hood was another story. New federal emissions requirements dictated that all 1971 cars had to be able to run on low-lead gasoline (87 octane). To comply, Chevrolet dropped the compression in the Z28's 350 V-8 from 11:1 to 9:1. Horsepower dropped commensurately, from 360 to 330 gross. In addition, Chevrolet began listing horsepower in net figures as well; horsepower for the Z engine was pegged at 275 using that method.

The Z28 still presented a bold image; the broad twin stripes still ran from cowl to grille and from rear window to trunk lip, over the rear spoiler. Z28 emblems were emblazoned on the blacked out grille, the front fenders and on the center of the trunk lip just under the spoiler. Tires were massive F60-15s, mounted on 15x7 inch Trans Am wheels with chrome lug nuts, centers and trim rings. The F-41 suspension continued to provide superior handling. For 1971, positraction and power front disc brakes were included as part of the Z28 package, which listed for $786.75.

Newly available in 1971 was an optional three-piece large spoiler, adapted from the one used on Pontiac's Firebird Trans Am. It was taller than the standard spoiler and wrapped over the sides to meet the beltline just above the rear side marker lights. Transmission choices were still the four-speed manual or the three-range Turbo Hydramatic; the four-speed again featured Hurst linkage. Still restricted from the Z28 was air conditioning, along with any options

that conflicted with the package, such as wheels and tires or the SS option.

The SS engines suffered from the low-octane fuel requirement, too. The standard 350 engine was down to 270 hp (210 net) and the optional big-block 396 was rated at a mere 300 hp (260 net). The SS option came with F70-14 wide-oval tires mounted on 14x7 inch rims; the Z28 was still the only Camaro to come with 15-inch wheels and tires. The four-speed manual or three-range automatic transmission was required, whichever engine was chosen. Like the Z28 and the Sports Coupe, the SS could be paired with the Rally Sport option.

The Rally Sport package in 1971 continued to provide a dramatic flair to the Camaro, with its round driving-light style turn signals mounted in the catwalks between the grille and the headlights. Small bumperettes flanked the blacked out floating grille, which was circled by a body-color Endura surround. On non-SS and non-Z28 models, an "RS" emblem graced the steering wheel and "RALLY SPORT" chrome emblems adorned each front fender.

As with all other ponycars, sales of the 1971 Camaro dropped. Only 114,643 were produced, of which 8,377 were SS models and 4,862 were Z28s. There was serious talk of dropping the Camaro (and its sister, the Firebird), but production of the 1972 model went ahead.

The 1971 Camaro catalogue was similar to the 1970 edition (see pages 70-65). The sporty Camaros were nicely covered in the large full-line Chevy accessories catalogue (see pages 66-67). An interesting "Road & Track" review was also reprinted and distributed through dealers (see page 68). The various Camaro-related items used during research on this book appear in the montage below.

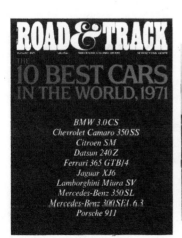

Before you go diving right into this page, hold on just one second. Flip the right page out.

There. Now, take a good long look at the Camaro Rally Sport.

Up front there's a blacked-out grille. It looks so big and mouthy, that it makes Camaro's wide stance seem even wider.

And it's surrounded with a resilient color-matched frame that acts as a bumper. Then there's a vertical bar down the middle of the grille. It's resilient, too (a special kind of rubber). So, if somebody gives you a klunk, chances are there'll be no bruises. And no hurt feelings.

But that's not all the bumper you get. There's a split-bumper that wraps clear around to both sides of the front end.

And see those lights? One's a rally-styled parking light. The other, Camaro's high-intensity headlight. They set the Rally Sport apart from other

cars. Even in the dark. (You can see it on the back page.)

RS

There are Hide-A-Way windshield wipers that tuck out of sight. Flared wheel openings like you see on expensive sports cars. Bucket seats. And bright styling accents—like the molding on the rear of the hood shown below—that give it looks on top of looks. Even the door handles are color accented to match the Magic-Mirror exterior hue.

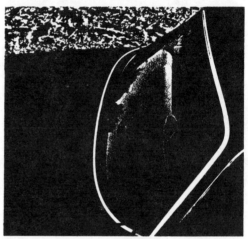

And on the steering wheel, there's a big, bright RS emblem so you always know you've got something special.

Just watch. When you pull up in this one, you'll get a lot more than admiring glances.

(Now, flip the right-hand page back, and this one out.)

SS

Now that you've seen both the RS and SS, here comes the big decision.

Which one you want more.

Go back. Take another look at both.

. . . . . . are you with us again?

Good. Now we'll fill you in on the SS. (Might help you make up your mind which one you like better.)

This is the car for you if you really look forward to getting behind the wheel. Even if it's just to visit somebody down the street.

The standard engine you get is a

270-horse 350-cubic-inch V8 that inhales through a 4-barrel carb and exhales through dual exhausts. If you want still more, you can order the 300-horse Turbo-Jet 396 V8. (Either one runs fine on low lead fuel.) When you order the 396 you get sport suspension with a special front stabilizer, rear stabilizer bar, special shock absorbers and black rear panel. Both SS V8s require 4-Speed or Turbo Hydra-matic. That way you've got all the horses in the palm of your hand.

With any SS you also get hood insulation, sport mirror and black grille. The rubber is white-lettered F70 x 14 on 7"-wide wheels. Disc/drum brakes are standard here, too, but with the SS they're power assisted.

And in case you couldn't find the windshield wipers, relax. They're the Hide-A-Way kind.

We've even added something for the benefit of other cars. Distinctive SS identification. That way they'll always know what they're up against.

But the best thing is, you don't have to be rich to make the scene.

When you go driving in this one, have the neighbors take your mail.

You might be gone for a while.

Camaro Sport Coupe with Z28 package and special spoiler.

Z28

This is the Camaro Z28. It's not for everybody.

We recommend it for the guy who always wanted a performance car that he could drive to work.

Let's start with the engine. It's a special 330-horse Turbo-Fire 350 V8. (Even this one takes low lead fuel.) And there's a lot that's special about it. Like the cam. The mechanical lifters. The big 4-barrel carb. Everything spells performance.

But there's more to it than that.

You also get special instrumentation. (See Options page.) Extruded aluminum pistons. Extra-large intake and exhaust valves. And a thermo-modulated fan that cuts in when the engine needs more cool.

Same thing with the transmission. Order 4-Speed with Hurst linkage and you get short crisp throws. If you want to go the automatic route, you can order the Turbo Hydra-matic. It's a three-range setup that shifts itself or lets you take over.

The suspension? Ditto. There are special shocks at all four wheels. A stabilizer bar in the rear as well as the front. And power disc/drum brakes. Combine all that with the Z28's quick-ratio steering and you'll move through corners flat and precise.

Then, there are other performance telltales. Special 15" x 7" wheels with F60 x 15 white-lettered tires. Heavy-duty radiator. Special Z28 striping. And a Positraction rear axle. Now, that's what we call a healthy car.

One more thing. The "Z" comes with a standard rear spoiler. Or, you can order special spoilers like the one shown opposite. See Options page.

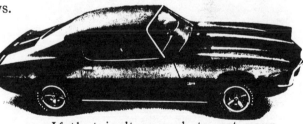

If that isn't enough to get your adrenaline flowing, there's a Corvette catalog not too far away.

Our things for yours.
Available Camaro Options.

Let's suppose somebody on the next block has a new Camaro, too. That's nice, but no two Camaros have to be exactly alike. Here's how you can do it up your way.

Special Spoilers

Expensive sports cars have spoilers like these. And you can order them on Camaro. One wraps around the rear deck. The other one's up front. And they work as good as they look.

Four-Season Air Conditioning

It's a nice thing to have when the heat's on outside. Adjust the controls, roll up the windows and enjoy the cool. (V8 models only.)

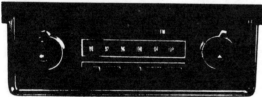

AM/FM Radio

The Camaro itself is entertaining enough. But some good sounds can make it better yet. And see those little lines in the windshield? That's the antenna. That's right, the antenna.

Special Instrumentation

Forget the tack-on tach. Ours is on the instrument panel, along with a temperature gauge and an ammeter. There's even a clock to show you what good times you're making.

Center Console

The action is right here whether you order manual or automatic transmissions. This neat setup has a big storage compartment and rear courtesy light.

Custom Interior

With such a great looking outside, why not order an extra special inside?

You can take your choice of cloth-vinyl buckets in five colors (black, black/blue, black/jade, black/saddle or black/white).

You also get simulated wood-grain accents on instrument cluster panel, door trim panels, steering wheel and center console when ordered. Plus extra body insulation, luggage compartment mat and more. Now, that's what we call plush.

Vinyl Roof Cover

Order this option and its like putting frosting on the cake. The vinyl roof comes in five color choices: black, white, dark blue, dark brown, dark green.

Your Chevy dealer has a complete list of Options and Custom Features.

Accident Prevention

Seat belts with pushbutton buckles for all passenger positions. Shoulder belts with pushbutton buckles—driver and right front passenger. Two built-in front seat head restraints. Energy-absorbing steering column. Passenger-guard door locks with forward-mounted door lock buttons. Safety door latches and hinges. Folding seat back latches. Energy-absorbing instrument panel and front seat back tops. Contoured roof rails. Thick-laminate windshield. Padded sun visors. Safety armrests. Safety steering wheel. Side-guard door beams. Cargo-guard luggage compartment.

Occupant Protection Features

Side marker lights and reflectors (front side marker lights flash with direction signal). Four-way hazard warning flasher. Backup lights. Lane-change feature in directional signal control. Windshield defroster, washers and dual-speed wipers. Wide-view inside day-night mirror (vinyl-edged shatter-resistant glass). Outside rearview mirror. Dual master cylinder brake system with warning light. Dual-action safety hood latches.

Anti-theft Features

Anti-theft ignition key warning buzzer. Anti-theft steering column lock.

CAMARO POWER TEAMS**					
	TRANSMISSIONS	REAR AXLE RATIOS	COMPRESSION RATIO	GROSS TORQUE	CARBURETION
STANDARD ENGINES					
145-hp (110-hp*) Turbo Thrift 250 Six	3-Speed	3.08	8.5:1	230 lb-ft/1600 rpm (185/1600*)	Single-barrel
	Powerglide	3.08			
200-hp (140-hp*) Turbo-Fire 307 V8	3-Speed	3.08	8.5:1	300 lb-ft/2400 rpm (235/2400*)	Two-barrel
	Powerglide	3.08			
	Turbo Hydra-matic	2.73			
AVAILABLE ENGINES					
245-hp (165-hp*) Turbo-Fire 350	4-Speed	3.08	8.5:1	350 lb-ft/2800 rpm (280/2400*)	Two-barrel
	Turbo Hydra-matic	2.73			
270-hp (210-hp*) Turbo-Fire 350 V8 (SS only)	4-Speed	3.42	8.5:1	360 lb-ft/3200 rpm (300/2800*)	Four-barrel
	Turbo Hydra-matic	3.08			
330-hp (275-hp*) Turbo-Fire 350 V8 (Z28 only)	4-Speed	3.73 or Special Option 4.10	9.0:1	360 lb-ft/4000 rpm (300/4000*)	Four-barrel
	Turbo Hydra-matic				
300-hp (260-hp*) Turbo-Jet 396 V8 (SS only)	4-Speed	3.42	8.5:1	400 lb-ft/3200 rpm (345/3200*)	Four-barrel
	Turbo Hydra-matic				

*S.A.E. net (as installed) rating.
**For 1971, all Camaro engines have been designed to operate efficiently on the new no-lead or low-lead gasolines. In addition to the lower exhaust emissions attainable with this engine/fuel combination, there are benefits in longer life for your spark plugs, exhaust system and other engine components. If these no-lead, low-lead gasolines are not available, any leaded regular grade gasoline with a research octane number of 91 or higher may be used.

Camaro RS. Includes special black grille with resilient vertical center bar and bright outline. Resilient grille frame. Separate left and right front bumpers. License plate mounting below right bumper. Roadlight-styled parking lights beside head-lights. Hide-A-Way windshield wipers. Bright molding on rear edge of hood. Bright window moldings. Color-accented door handles. Bright accents on parking lights and taillights. RS emblem on steering wheel. Rally Sport front fender nameplates.

Camaro RS

Camaro Style Trim Group (included in RS option). Includes bright molding on rear edge of hood. Bright window moldings. Color-accented door handles. Bright accents on parking lights and taillights.

Camaro Custom Interior. Available in five luxurious cloth and vinyl bucket seat choices—black, black/blue, black/jade, black/saddle or black/white. Molded vinyl door panels with simulated wood-grain trim, bright accent moldings and carpeted lower edge. Additional instrument cluster lighting. Glove compartment light. Simulated wood-grain accents on instrument cluster and steering wheel. Special body insulation. Luggage compartment mat.

Camaro Interior Accent Group (included in Custom Interior option). Additional instrument cluster lighting. Simulated wood-grain accents on instrument panel and steering wheel.

Camaro SS

Camaro Z28

Camaro SS. Black grille with bright outline. Hide-A-Way windshield wipers. Left-hand remote-controlled Sport Mirror. SS emblem on steering wheel, grille and fenders. Special ornamentation. Option also includes: 270 (210)-hp Turbo-Fire 350 or extra-cost 300 (260)-hp Turbo-Jet 396. Special hood insulation. Power brakes. Bright engine accents. 14 x 7 wheels. White-lettered F70 x 14 bias belted ply tires. Dual exhaust system with bright outlets. Sport Suspension included with 300 (260)-hp Turbo-Jet 396 V8 option.

Camaro Z28. Includes black grille with bright outline. Wide rally stripes on hood and rear deck. Left-hand remote-controlled Sport Mirror. Air spoiler on rear deck. Z28 emblem on grille, front fenders and rear deck spoiler. Rear bumper guards. Special 15 x 7 wheels with bright wheel nuts. White-lettered F60 x 15 bias belted ply tires. Option also includes: Special 330 (275)-hp Turbo-Fire 350-cu.-in. V8 engine. Special instrumentation. Special front and rear springs. Sport Suspension. Bright engine accents. Heavy-duty radiator. Power brakes. Positraction rear axle. Dual exhaust system with bright outlets. Note: Z28 equipment available for V8 model only when either 4-Speed or Turbo Hydra-matic transmission is ordered. Air conditioning, wheel covers and Rally Wheels are not available for Camaro Z28.

This section describes the many available Chevrolet model options. Where the model includes an optional engine, horsepower figures in parentheses indicate SAE net horsepower, as installed.

Camaro 350SS
ONE OF THE TEN BEST CARS IN THE WORLD, 1971. ALSO BEST SEDAN, $4000–6000.

THE CHEVROLET Camaro proves that Detroit can build a good, esthetically pleasing road car for a reasonable price. Its classification as a sedan is somewhat equivocal; we could have easily called it a Sports/GT, but whatever the category, it is an outstanding car. Chevrolet engineers seriously tried to incorporate in it some lessons learned from European GTs and in doing so gave it adequate suspension, standard front disc brakes, a good driving position and wide wheels and tires. Meanwhile, the stylists were giving it an astonishingly beautiful body, albeit an overlarge and not particularly space-efficient one. But for less than $5000 one can buy a Camaro 350SS and it's one great hunk of car for that money.

1972

1972 was almost the last year for the Camaro; a strike at the Norwood, Ohio plant, where all Camaros and Firebirds were made, lasted for half of the year. Because the strike ran very close to the time to gear up for the 1973 models and because ponycar sales in general were continuing to drop some executives thought it might be better to discontinue the line. Fortunately, they were in the minority and the decision to continue won out. Still, 1,100 partially completed Camaros had to be scrapped at the end of the strike because they could not be modified to conform to the new 1973 federal safety requirements.

The only visual change to the 1972 Camaro was on the non-Rally Sport models; the grid in the grille was a coarser mesh. But the feds continued to take their toll, as power ratings again dropped on all engines.

The Z28 engine was now rated at 255 hp, down from 275 in 1971, but still the strongest engine offered in any Camaro. It had to be teamed with one of the three four-speed transmissions, which now featured a positive reverse lockout mechanism in the linkage, or the three-range automatic. Included in the package were the F-41 handling suspension; F60x15 raised-letter wide-oval tires mounted on 15x7 inch Trans Am rims with chrome centers, lug nuts and trim rings; positraction; dual sports mirrors; and Z28 emblems on the grille, front fenders and the trunk lip. The standard small spoiler was dropped and the large, three-piece spoiler was combined with a front spoiler as RPO D-80. The famous dual wide stripes were made a delete option; they came with the package, but you could order the car without them. Engine dress-up items consisted of finned aluminum valve covers and a chromed air cleaner cover. To handle the strongest Camaro engine, the Z28 package included heavy-duty starter, radiator and engine mounts. Dropped from the Z28 package was the fast-ratio steering, but it was optionally available.

The SS option featured a 350 engine rated at only 200 hp; the optional big-block engine was still called the 396, although it had been stroked to 402 cubic inches and was rated at 240 hp. The engine size was indicated on the front fenders, just under the "SS" emblems. The SS only came with 14-inch rims fitted with 70-series wide-oval tires; the Z28 was still the only Camaro that came with 15-inchers.

Again for 1972, the Rally Sport package could be combined with the base Sport Coupe, the SS and the Z28 packages. It still featured the round turn signals mounted in the catwalks between the grille and the headlights. The blacked out grille now had argent accents both horizontally and vertically and was again circled by a body color surround, with bumperettes flanking it.

All 1972 Camaros are rare because of the strike-shortened production year; only 68,656 were built. And a 1972 Z28 is very hard to find because there were only 2,575 of them made.

The 1972 Camaro catalogue was a new design from the 1970-71 versions (see pages 70-78).

The Rally

Take a Camaro Sport Coupe, add the Rally Sport package, and you've got a different looking Camaro.

Rally Sport is mainly an appearance package to make Camaro look even sportier than the

standard version.

The first RS feature people notice is the dent-resistant frame which surrounds the grille. It's painted the same color as the body and helps resist dings and nicks, especially in parking spots.

Rally Sport nameplate on fenders.

Sport Camaro.

Below is the Rally Sport Camaro. And everything that goes with it.

This Rally Sport Camaro is also equipped with our Style Trim Group which includes: bright belt molding, bright rear pillar molding, bright accents on taillights and parking lights, bright roof drip moldings, and bright molding on the rear edge of the hood and body-color door handle accents.

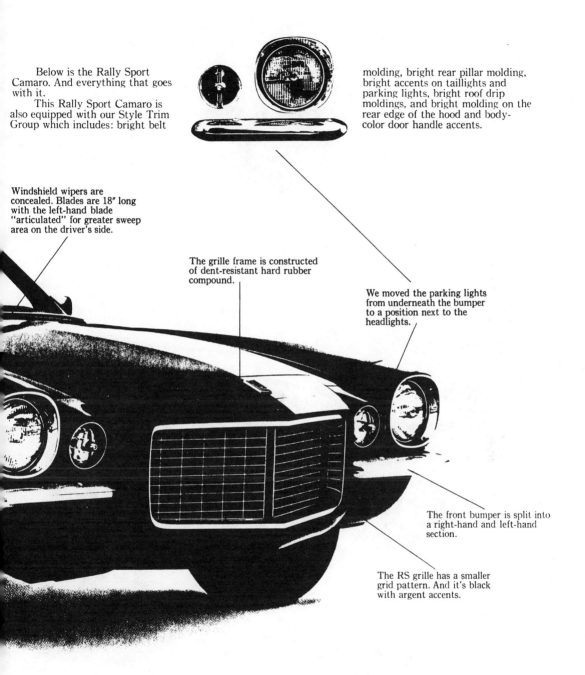

Windshield wipers are concealed. Blades are 18″ long with the left-hand blade "articulated" for greater sweep area on the driver's side.

The grille frame is constructed of dent-resistant hard rubber compound.

We moved the parking lights from underneath the bumper to a position next to the headlights.

The front bumper is split into a right-hand and left-hand section.

The RS grille has a smaller grid pattern. And it's black with argent accents.

The Super

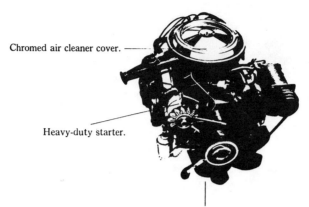

Chromed air cleaner cover. ⸺

Heavy-duty starter.

200-hp Turbo-Fire 350 V8. Or
available 240-hp Turbo-Jet
396 V8.

If a little more performance
is what you're looking for, we have
the answer in our available
SS package.
   Except for a few obvious
things, like Hide-A-Way windshield
wipers and a black grille, most of
the features in the SS package are

Special hood insulation.

Hide-A-Way windshield wipers.

Heavy-duty radiator.

SS grille emblem.

Black grille.

With 396 V8: sport suspension,
heavier duty front stabilizer
bar, rear stabilizer bar, and
special front and rear shock
absorbers.

Power brakes.

Heavy-duty clutch.
Available transmissions: 4-Speed
(2.54:1 low with 350 V8; 2.52:1 low
with 396 V8). Close-ratio 4-Speed
(2.20:1 low, 396 V8 only).
Turbo Hydra-matic.

Sport Camaro.

hidden underneath Camaro's
sleek body.
But just drive the SS onto
a stretch of winding road and
you'll feel those hidden features.
Here's how the SS reads out.

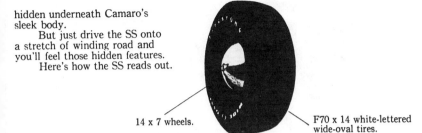

14 x 7 wheels.

F70 x 14 white-lettered
wide-oval tires.

Remote-control sport mirror.

This SS is equipped with front
and rear spoilers (both available
on all Camaro models).

Black rear panel
(with 396
V8 only).

Dual exhaust system.

SS fender emblem.
Engine size numerals.

Heavy-duty driveline
universal joints.

The Z28

From its special 15 x 7 wheels to the twin rally stripes on the hood and trunk, our Z28 Camaro is all performance.

There's a special engine available only in this Camaro. It's the only Camaro with 15-inch wheels.

Dual exhaust system.

Z28 emblem on trunk lid.

Special instrumentation package including a tach, ammeter, temperature gauge and clock.

Right-hand sport mirror.

Remote-control sport mirror.

Rear stabilizer bar.

Z28 fender emblem.

Positraction rear axle with 3.73:1 ratio.

Heavy-duty driveline universal joints.

Power brakes.

Special front and rear shock absorbers.

Heavy-duty clutch.

Camaro.

It has a new shifter featuring a positive reverse lockout with the 4-Speed.

We put a little something special into this Camaro. So you could get a little something special out of it.

15 x 7 wheels with bright lug nuts, special center caps and trim rings.

Available transmissions: 4-Speed (2.52:1 low). Close-ratio 4-Speed (2.20:1 low). Special close-ratio 4-Speed (2.20:1 low). Special quick-shifting Turbo Hydra-matic.

F60 x 15 white-lettered wide-oval tires.

Special 255-hp Turbo-Fire 350 V8 with extruded aluminum pistons, extra-large valves, special flex fan, special-performance cam, mechanical lifters and a big 4-barrel carb.

Rally stripes on the hood and trunk lid.

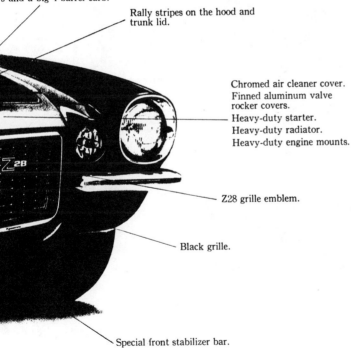

Chromed air cleaner cover.
Finned aluminum valve rocker covers.
Heavy-duty starter.
Heavy-duty radiator.
Heavy-duty engine mounts.

Z28 grille emblem.

Black grille.

Special front stabilizer bar.

Camaro

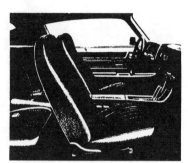

Custom Interior. Cloth and vinyl seats in black, black/blue, black/green and black/covert. Simulated wood-grain accents on upper door panel and instrument cluster.

Wheel Covers. Two styles to order from.

Remote-Control Sport Mirror. Driver's side mirror adjusts with a handy switch on the door panel. Right-hand sport mirror also available.

Front and Rear Spoilers. Include lower front spoiler and a special full-width rear spoiler that extends down sides of rear fenders. Both spoilers add to Camaro's handling, especially at highway speeds.

New "Wet Look" Vinyl Roof. Comes in black, white, green, covert and tan. Black and white available with all exterior colors. Others available depending on exterior color.

Floor Console. Mounts between front bucket seats. Contains storage compartment, ashtray for rear passengers and houses transmission shift lever when ordered.

Special Instrumentation. Includes tachometer, ammeter, temperature gauge, electric clock.

Extras.

Four-Season Air Conditioning.
Turns the Camaro interior into
your own private environment.
Cools, filters as you like it.

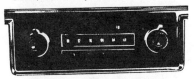

AM/FM Radio. Pushbutton
operation. Includes antenna
concealed in windshield.

Rally Wheels. Wide 14 x 7
wheels are available with any
Camaro model.

Other Extras.

Two-position adjustable
driver's seat back. Heavy-duty
battery. Deluxe seat and shoulder
belts. Deluxe front and rear
bumpers. Soft-Ray tinted glass.
Auxiliary lighting including
courtesy lights, glove box light,
luggage compartment light, ashtray
light and underhood light. Heavy-
duty radiator. AM pushbutton
radio. Rear-seat speaker. Comfortilt
steering wheel (with automatic
transmission only). Sport suspension.
Hide-A-Way windshield wipers.
Power brakes. Variable-ratio power
steering. Interior Accent Group:
includes simulated wood-grain
accents on the instrument panel and
additional instrument cluster
lighting. Operating Convenience
Group: includes electric clock and
rear window defroster. Appearance
Guard Group: includes door edge
guards, color-keyed floor mats and
visor vanity mirror.

Some of these extras are
standard equipment with certain
Camaro Option Packages. Check
with your Chevrolet dealer. He also
offers a long list of Custom Features
for Camaro, such as a stereo
cartridge tape player, fire
extinguisher, hood lock pins, ski
rack, wire and mag-style wheel
covers, and many more. See your
dealer for information.

Camaro Power Teams

Engine	SAE net horsepower	Carburetion	Transmission	Rear axle ratio*
STANDARD				
Turbo-Thrift 250 250-cu.-in. Six	110	Single-barrel	3-Speed (2.85:1 low) Powerglide	3.08
Turbo-Fire 307 307-cu.-in. V8	130	Two-barrel	3-Speed (2.85:1 low) Powerglide	3.08
			Turbo Hydra-matic	2.73†
AVAILABLE				
Turbo-Fire 350 350-cu.-in. V8	165	Two-barrel	3-Speed (2.54:1 low)# 4-Speed (2.54:1 low)	3.08
			Turbo Hydra-matic	2.73†
Turbo-Fire 350 350-cu.-in. V8 (SS only)	200	Four-barrel	4-Speed (2.54:1 low)	3.42
			Turbo Hydra-matic	3.08
Turbo-Fire 350 350-cu.-in. V8 (Z28 only)	255	Four-barrel	4-Speed (2.52:1 low) 4-Speed (2.20:1 low) Heavy-Duty 4-Speed (2.20:1 low) Turbo Hydra-matic	3.73**
Turbo-Jet 396†† 402-cu.-in. V8 (SS only)	240	Special Four-barrel	4-Speed (2.52:1 low) 4-Speed (2.20:1 low) Turbo Hydra-matic	3.42

*Positraction required for 3.73 and 410
ratios. Available for all others.
**4.10 performance ratio available.
†3.42 trailering ratio available.
††Not available in California.
#This power team available only with
California emission system

For 1972, all Camaro engines have been designed to operate
efficiently on the new low-lead or no-lead gasolines. In addition to the
lower exhaust pollutants attainable with this engine/fuel combination,
there are benefits in longer life for your spark plugs, exhaust system
and other engine components. If these no-lead, low-lead gasolines
are not available, any leaded regular grade gasoline with a research
octane number of 91 or higher may be used.

We want your new Camaro to be the best car you ever owned.

Model
☐ Sport Coupe
☐ Rally Sport
☐ SS
☐ Z28

Interior
☐ Standard Interior
☐ Interior Accent Group
☐ Custom Interior

Engines
☐ 110-hp Turbo-Thrift 250 Six
☐ 130-hp Turbo-Fire 307 V8
☐ 165-hp Turbo-Fire 350 V8
☐ 200-hp Turbo-Fire 350 V8 (SS only)
☐ 255-hp Turbo-Fire 350 V8 (Z28 only)
☐ 240-hp Turbo-Jet 396 V8 (SS only)

Transmissions
☐ 3-Speed
☐ 4-Speed
☐ Powerglide
☐ Turbo Hydra-matic

Popular Extras
☐ Sport mirrors
☐ Wheel covers
☐ Sport suspension
☐ Soft-Ray tinted glass
☐ Center console
☐ Four-Season air conditioning
☐ Power brakes
☐ Variable-ratio power steering
☐ AM/FM radio
☐ Front and rear air spoilers
☐ "Wet-look" vinyl roof cover
☐ Operating Convenience Group including electric clock and rear window defroster.

☐ Appearance Guard Group including door edge guards, color-keyed floor mats and visor vanity mirror.

Magic-Mirror Colors
☐ Mulsanne Blue ☐ Midnight Bronze ☐ Mohave Gold ☐ Placer Gold ☐ Ascot Blue ☐ Gulf Green ☐ Sequoia Green ☐ Spring Green ☐ Orange Flame ☐ Cranberry Red ☐ Pewter Silver ☐ Covert Tan ☐ Antique White ☐ Cream Yellow ☐ Golden Brown

Camaro Specifications
Dimensions

Wheelbase................108.0"
Overall length.............188.0"
Overall width................74.4"
Tread—front................*61.3"
　　　—rear.................*60.0"
*SS—front..................61.6"
　　—rear..................60.3"
Z28—front..................61.7"
　　—rear..................60.4"
Overall height..............49.1"
Head room—front..........37.4"
　　　　—rear..........36.1"
Leg room—front...........43.8"
　　　　—rear...........30.7"
Hip room—front...........53.3"
　　　　—rear...........47.2"
Shoulder room—front.......57.4"
　　　　　—rear.......54.4"

Capacities

Gas tank (approx.)..........18 gal.
Oil.......................4 qts.
Usable luggage space.....6.4 cu. ft.

Camaro Safety and Security Features
Occupant Protection. Seat belts with pushbutton buckles for all passenger positions. Shoulder belts with pushbutton buckles—driver and right front passenger. Two built-in front seat head restraints. Energy-absorbing steering column. Passenger-guard door locks with forward-mounted lock buttons. Safety door latches and hinges. Folding seat back latches. Energy-absorbing padded instrument panel and front seat back tops. Thick-laminate windshield. Padded sun visors. Safety armrests. Safety steering wheel. Side-guard beams. Cargo guard luggage compartment. Fuel tank impact security. Contoured full roof inner panel.

Accident Prevention. Side marker lights and reflectors. Parking lights that illuminate with headlights. Four-way hazard warning flasher. Backup lights. Lane-change feature in direction signal control. Windshield defroster, washers and dual-speed wipers. Wide-view inside day-night mirror (vinyl-edged, shatter-resistant glass and deflecting support). Outside rearview mirror. Dual master cylinder brake system with warning light. Starter safety switch. Dual-action safety hood latches.

Anti-Theft. Anti-theft ignition key warning buzzer. Anti-theft steering column lock. Visible vehicle identification.

Building a better way to see the U.S.A.

All illustrations and specifications contained in this literature are based on the latest product information available at the time of publication approval. The right is reserved to make changes at any time without notice in prices, colors, materials, equipment, specifications and models and to discontinue models. Chevrolet Motor Division, General Motors Corporation, Detroit, Michigan 48202.

To many auto enthusiasts, Big Brother struck eleven years ahead of George Orwell's prediction. New federal regulations seemed destined to take the performance and joy out of cars.

As an example, instead of trying to make the big-block engine comply with emission requirements, Chevrolet dropped it from the Camaro lineup. In fact, they dropped the whole SS option. The Z28 was sole heir to the Camaro performance image.

To replace the SS, Chevrolet introduced the Type LT. This was an upscale model with the emphasis on posh instead of performance. The standard LT engine was a watered-down version of the 350, putting out a modest 145 hp. The emphasis was on trim and niceties, with luxury-look fabrics and a multitude of light packages and sound deadening to lend an air of plushness.

The 350 engine in the Z28 suffered another loss of power; it was now rated at 245 hp as opposed to the 255 hp of 1972. Still, there was enough there to get the adrenaline pumping. Hydraulic lifters replaced the solid type that had been fitted since the Z was born. The aluminum manifold was dropped and the Holley four-barrel carburetor was replaced by a Rochester Quadrajet. Only two four-speed manual transmissions were available this year: wide or close ratio; the Turbo Hydramatic three-speed was available

for those who preferred to go clutchless. Still included in the Z28 package were the F-41 suspension, positraction, 15x7 inch Trans Am wheels fitted with F60x15 raised-letter wide-oval tires and power brakes. The stripes still came with it, but they could be deleted on request. For the first time, air conditioning could be ordered on a Z28. The D-80 spoiler option consisted of the three-piece unit on the back and the small air dam for the front. The price of the Z28 option was dropped to $502 for 1973. As in previous years, the Rally Sport option could be ordered on the Z28.

The Rally Sport package continued to be a good looking addition to the Camaro. It still featured the turn signals mounted in the catwalks between the grille and the headlights. The grille was a floating style with bright vertical and horizontal accenting. It was circled by a body-color hard rubber surround and flanked by bumperettes.

Sales of all ponycars continued to slide and the Camaro was no different. For the whole 1973 model year only 96,756 Camaros were made. Of that number, 11,574 were Z28s.

The 1973 Camaro catalogue was similar in size to the 1969-72 editions, but once again the format was revised (see pages 80-82).

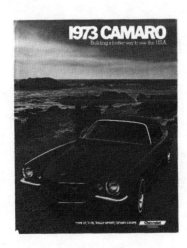

The Rally Sport. The available Rally Sport package is designed to add a different look to any Camaro.

Rally Sport includes a special black grille with silver accents. And Rally Sport nameplates just behind the front wheel wells.

The grille itself is surrounded by a resilient frame which helps guard against minor dings and dents. On either side of the grille are small "bumperettes."

To maintain the clean look of the grille, the license plate mounting is below the right bumper.

The parking lights are moved from under the bumper to a position next to the headlights and take on a road-light style.

Rally Sport also features Hide-A-Way windshield wipers.

The Rally Sport package can be ordered with the standard Camaro Sport Coupe, Type LT or the Z28.

The Camaro Z28. Better known simply as "The Z". It's for those who demand a little more performance.

The Z28 features a new Turbo-Fire Special 350-4 V8 engine with a 4-barrel carburetor and dual exhaust system. This engine has hydraulic valve lifters and includes a new

open-element air cleaner for a sound you have to hear to appreciate. And like all Chevrolet engines, it runs on regular, no-lead or low-lead gas.

The Z28 is available with either of two manual 4-Speeds or Turbo Hydra-matic. Air conditioning is available with the Z28 for the first

time. You can also order the front and rear spoilers shown above.

Other "Z" features, all standard: sport suspension, special 15 x 7 wheels and F60 x 15 white lettered tires, power brakes, Positraction, a black-finish grille, sport mirrors on both sides and Z28 identification.

Camaro Sport Coupe

Camaro Z28

Camaro Type LT.

Camaro Rally Sport

Use this handy check list as an order guide for your 1973 Camaro.
- [ ] Sport Coupe
- [ ] Z28
- [ ] Type LT
- [ ] Rally Sport equipment

- [ ] Turbo-Thrift 250 Six
- [ ] Turbo-Fire 307 V8
- [ ] Turbo-Fire 350-2 V8
- [ ] Turbo-Fire 350-4 V8
- [ ] Turbo-Fire Special 350-4 V8 (Z28 only)

- [ ] 3-Speed
- [ ] 4-Speed Wide-Range
- [ ] 4-Speed Close-Ratio (Z28 only)
- [ ] Turbo Hydra-matic

- [ ] Four-Season air conditioning
- [ ] Soft-Ray tinted glass
- [ ] Center console
- [ ] Power steering
- [ ] Power brakes
- [ ] AM radio
- [ ] AM/FM radio
- [ ] Vinyl roof
- [ ] Color-keyed floor mats
- [ ] Rear window defroster
- [ ] Door edge guards
- [ ] Sport mirrors
- [ ] Electric clock
- [ ] Special instrumentation
- [ ] Rally Wheels
- [ ] Turbine I Wheels
- [ ] Wire wheel covers

- [ ] Light Blue Metallic
- [ ] Dark Blue Metallic
- [ ] Midnight Blue Metallic
- [ ] Dark Brown Metallic
- [ ] Chamois
- [ ] Light Copper Metallic
- [ ] Green-Gold Metallic
- [ ] Light Green Metallic
- [ ] Dark Green Metallic
- [ ] Midnight Green
- [ ] Medium Orange Metallic
- [ ] Medium Red
- [ ] Dark Red Metallic
- [ ] Silver Metallic
- [ ] Antique White
- [ ] Light Yellow

All illustrations and specifications contained in this literature are based on the latest product information available at the time of publication approval. The right is reserved to make changes at any time without notice, in prices, colors, materials, equipment, specifications and models, and to discontinue models. Chevrolet Motor Division, General Motors Corporation, Detroit, Michigan 48202. Litho in U.S.A.

An important change occurred in all cars sold in the U.S. in 1974. The Federal Government, in its best Big Brother attitude, mandated several restrictions on top of the ones they had been imposing since 1966. The most notorious, and the biggest failure, was the ignition interlock. The idea was to require the driver's (and front-seat passenger's, if someone was sitting there) seat belt to be fastened before the car could be started. The means to accomplish this task was a switch built into the seat belt mechanism, plus a sensor in the seat to determine if someone was sitting on it. There are many stories about people who tried, and often beat, these maniacal contraptions. A lot of mechanically inclined people made money by secretly disconnecting or bypassing them; nobody would admit to it, though, because it was illegal. The regulation, unpopular with so many people, was quickly repealed. Only the 1974 models were afflicted and it is a rare 1974 model that still has an active system.

Another gift from Big Brother that year was the five-mph-impact-absorbing bumpers. Many different styles were used; some were more successful than others. Esthetics on some cars suffered because of those bumpers, but the Camaro came out looking pretty good.

The Camaro was restyled to help blend the bumper into the lines of the car. A one-piece nose was fitted that integrated the grille, headlights and turn signals into a forward-and-down slope to the bumper. The headlights and turn signals were deeply recessed into what came to be called "sugar scoops."

Taillights were changed from the Corvette-like bullets to single lenses that wrapped around the edges of the car to include side markers.

The Rally Sport option was dropped that year, leaving the Sport Coupe, Type LT and Z28. As in 1973, the Z28 could be order on the Type LT or the base Sport Coupe.

The engine in the Z28 was still rated at 245 hp, and the transmission choices were still three: a wide-range or close-ratio four-speed manual, or the three-speed automatic. Also included in the package were the F-41 suspension, positraction, 15x7 inch Trans Am wheels fitted with F60x15 wide-oval tires, heavy-duty starter and radiator, power brakes with discs at the front, dual sport mirrors and dual exhausts. New for 1974 were a high-energy ignition and a dual snorkel air intake.

The graphics were changed for 1974 as well. Gone were the familiar dual wide stripes on the hood and trunk lid, replaced by a huge white field with three broad black stripes running from cowl to front lip on the hood and down the length of the trunk lid. At the front and back, the stripes terminated in the letters "Z," "2," and "8": one on each stripe. Fortunately, they were a delete option and a lot of people elected to do without them. The D-80 option included the front air dam and the three-piece rear spoiler, and was quite popular.

Sales of Camaros were up for 1974. A total of 151,008 were built and 13,802 of them were Z28s.

The 1974 Camaro catalogue was similar to the 1973 edition (see pages 84-88).

Z28

In a word: Performance. In two words: Go bananas!
This is the Camaro for people who are sincerely interested in cars and really enjoy driving. Things like wide wheels, long hood, downshifting and tricky "S" curve after tricky "S" curve. Who've even been known to stick their heads in the engine compartment to see how things are going.

Standard Z28 engine: Our 350 V8 with four-barrel carburetor.

Also standard: New High-Energy Ignition System that eliminates conventional points and coil. Dual exhaust system. New dual-snorkel air cleaner. Special sport suspension system. Wide 15 x 7 wheels with lug nuts. center caps and trim rings. F60-15 bias belted white lettered tires. Heavy-duty starter. Increased cooling. Variable-ratio power steering. Power brakes. Positraction rear axle. Right- and left-side aerodynamic outside sport mirrors. With those famous Z28 spoilers available both coming and going.

And there's nothing bashful about the big, bold new stripes you can order with your Z28 package.

If you want a little more than the next person in the way a car moves, move out in a Z.

Left: The Z28 itself with available stripes and spoilers.

Special 15 x 7 wheels with lug nuts, center caps and trim rings. Also, F60-15 bias belted white lettered tires.

Z28's 350 4-barrel V8.

FEATU

ON ALL CAMAROS

STANDARD

Ride and handling.
Independent front coil suspension smoothness • Multi-leaf rear springs with bias-mounted shock absorbers for comfort and traction • Body springs computer-selected to the weight of the Camaro you order • Variable-ratio power steering when you order a V8 engine • Crisp-handling forward-mounted steering linkage • Wide tread, large rim tires and wheels • Front disc brakes that resist the effects of water.

Power. Turbo-Thrift 250 Six (Sport Coupe only) or 350 V8 (Sport Coupe or Type LT) • 3-Speed manual transmission • New larger fuel tank

• Corrosion-fighting sealed side-terminal battery • Coolant recovery system protects against radiator fluid loss.

Durability. All-welded, quiet Body by Fisher • Rust-fighting inner fender liners • Self-cleaning rocker panels • Magic-Mirror acrylic lacquer finish in 16 colors.

Comfort. Full-foam molded Strato-bucket seats • Four-spoke, soft-rim sport steering wheel • New cut-pile carpeting door to door • Flow-through ventilation system for continuous supply of outside air • Double-panel steel roof.

Convenience.
Slam-and-lock doors • Improved jacking method with new bumper slots, front and rear • New combination seat and shoulder belt system with inertia reel allows driver and right front passenger freedom of movement. A new sequential starter interlock system helps you remember to use the new belt system.

Styling. Dramatically designed upper grille with matching lower grille • Long, sloping hood • New road-type parking lights • Wide, wrap-around rear taillights • Flush-fit, smooth door handles • Large curved side windows • Ten vinyl roof colors are available—six new for 1974 • Newly designed aluminum hubcaps (Sport Coupe only) • Single-unit power beam headlights recessed into front fenders • Bright anodized aluminum bumpers with black rubber impact strips.

Occupant protection. Seat belts with pushbutton buckles for all passenger positions • Two combination seat and shoulder belts for driver and right front passenger (with reminder light and buzzer, inertia reel and starter interlock) • Two built-in front seat head restraints • Energy-absorbing steering column • Passenger-

POWER TEAMS

Engines	Power Rating*	Carb./ Exh.**	3-Speed	4-Speed	Turbo Hydra-matic
Camaro Sport Coupe:				Not	
Turbo-Thrift 250 Six. Std. (1)	100	1/SE	Std.	Avail.	Avail.
Turbo-Fire 350-2 V8. Std. (2, 4)	145	2/SE	Std.	Avail.	Avail.
Turbo-Fire 350-4 V8. Avail. (3, 4)	160	4/SE	Std.	Avail.	Avail.
Turbo-Fire 350-4 V8. Avail. (1, 4)	185	4/DE	Std.	Avail.	Avail.
Type LT Coupe:					
Turbo-Fire 350-2 V8. Std. (2, 4)	145	2/SE	Std.	Avail.	Avail.
Turbo-Fire 350-4 V8. Avail. (3, 4)	160	4/SE	Std.	Avail.	Avail.
Turbo-Fire 350-4 V8. Avail. (1, 4)	185	4/DE	Std.	Avail.	Avail.
Z28 Model Option:					
Turbo-Fire				Avail.	
Special 350-4 V8. Avail. (1)	245	4/DE	—	(5)	Avail.

*The horsepowers shown here are SAE net (as installed) ratings.
**First number indicates number of carburetor barrels, followed by letters for Single Exhaust or Dual Exhaust.

(1) California Emission Equipment required in State of California.
(2) Not available in California.
(3) Available only when California Emission Equipment is ordered.
(4) Available only with power brakes.
(5) Close-Ratio 4-Speed (RPO M21) also available except with air conditioning.

All 1974 Camaro engines are equipped with advanced exhaust emission control systems, and are designed to operate efficiently on unleaded or low-lead fuels of at least 91 Research Octane. In addition to the lower exhaust emissions attainable, there are benefits in longer life for your spark plugs, exhaust system and other engine components. If these unleaded, low-leaded gasolines are not available, any leaded 91 Research Octane or higher regular grade fuel containing 0.5 grams, or less, of lead per gallon should be used.

Camaro vital statistics: Wheelbase—108". Overall length—195.4". Height loaded—49.1". Front tread—61.3". Rear tread—60.0". Front head room—37.3". Rear head room—36.0". Front hip room—56.7". Rear hip room—47.3". Front shoulder room—56.7". Rear shoulder room—54.4". Front leg room—43.9". Rear leg room—29.6".

guard door locks • Safety door latches and hinges • Folding seat back latches • Energy-absorbing padded instrument panel and front seat back tops • Contoured windshield header • Thick-laminate windshield • Padded sun visors • Safety armrests • Safety steering wheel • Cargo-guard luggage compartment • Contoured full roof inner panel • Side-guard door beams.

Accident prevention. Side marker lights and reflectors (front side marker lights flash with direction signal) • Parking lights that illuminate with headlights • Four-way hazard warning flasher • Back-up lights • Lane-change feature in direction signal control • Windshield defroster, washers and dual-speed wipers • Wide-view inside day-night mirror (vinyl-edged, shatter-resistant glass and deflecting support) • Outside rearview mirror • Dual master cylinder brake system with warning light • Starter safety switch • Dual-action safety hood latch • Improved bumper system.

Anti-theft. Anti-theft ignition key warning buzzer • Anti-theft steering column lock.

More Type LT standards.
Luxury-Touring features. Interior Decor/Quiet Sound

Group with sound deadeners and insulation • Map pocket in each door • Deeper contoured front seat design • Ribbed cloth or knit-vinyl upholstery • Simulated Meridian Walnut interior accents • Special instrumentation including tachometer, ammeter, temperature gauge and electric clock • Variable-ratio power steering • Dual sport mirrors —LH remote • Hidden wind-shield wipers • Bright moldings around grille • Black-accented body side molding • Rally wheels • Turbo-Fire 350 V8 engine.

More things included with the Z28 package. (Z28 is available on either Sport Coupe or Type LT.)

Special 350 4-barrel V8 • New High-Energy Ignition System • New dual-snorkel air cleaner • Aluminized dual-exhaust system • Positraction rear axle • Special sport suspension components • Special 15 x 7 wheels • F60 x 15 bias belted white lettered tires • Heavy-duty starter • Additional cooling • Power brakes • Dual sport mirrors— driver's side remote-controlled.

Put together your own Camaro from this handy check list.

Model
☐ Sport Coupe
☐ Type LT

Available package
☐ Z28

Powered by
☐ Turbo-Thrift 250 Six (Sport Coupe only)
☐ Turbo-Fire 350-2 V8 (not available in California)
☐ Turbo-Fire 350-4 V8
☐ Turbo-Fire Special 350-4 V8 (Z28 only)

With
☐ 3-Speed (standard)
☐ 4-Speed wide-range
☐ 4-Speed close-ratio (Z28 only)
☐ Turbo Hydra-matic

Color
☐ Cream Beige
☐ Bright Blue Metallic
☐ Midnight Blue Metallic
☐ Aqua Blue Metallic
☐ Sandstone
☐ Bronze Metallic
☐ Golden Brown Metallic
☐ Lime Yellow
☐ Bright Yellow

☐ Light Gold Metallic
☐ Medium Red
☐ Bright Green Metallic
☐ Medium Dark Green Metallic
☐ Medium Red Metallic
☐ Silver Metallic
☐ Antique White

Upholstery

Sport Coupe:
☐ All-vinyl in
　☐ Black. ☐ Green.
　☐ Saddle. ☐ Red.
　☐ Neutral.
☐ Vinyl with cloth seat material in
　☐ Black with Black-White. ☐ Saddle with Saddle-Black. ☐ Green with Green-Black.

Type LT:
☐ All-vinyl in
　☐ Black. ☐ Saddle.
　☐ Taupe.
☐ Vinyl with ribbed-cloth seat material in
　☐ Black.
　☐ Saddle.
　☐ Neutral.
　☐ Taupe.

Now check the Options you'd like to order from the back cover.

OPTIONS

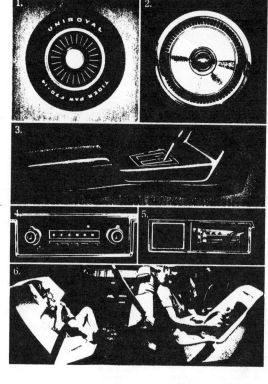

☐ 1. Turbine I wheels. The appearance of more costly cast aluminum wheels. (Not available with Z28.)
Also shown:
☐ F70-14 bias belted white lettered or white stripe tires. (Included: 14 x 7 wheels.)
☐ 2. Full wheel covers. (Sport Coupe only.)
☐ 3. Center console. Floor-mounted shift lever housing. Used as a roomy storage compartment, too.
☐ 4. AM/FM Stereo radio. Pushbutton, solid-state; matched set of speakers. Other AM or AM/FM (illustrated) single-speaker radios with pushbutton tuning also available.
☐ 5. Four-Season air conditioning. Newly redesigned for 1974. Wide-range control —cools, heats, defrosts and defogs. 61-amp. generator included.
☐ 6. GM Love Seats. Foam-padded, rugged polypropylene. Use car seat belt. Two sizes: infants and children.
☐ Steel belted radial ply tires. Blackwall, white stripe or white lettered FR78-14.
☐ Space-Saver spare tire. E78-14 or F78-14.
☐ Bold new sport striping. (Z28 only.)
☐ Power steering. (Included with V8 models.)
☐ Power brakes. (Included with Z28.)
☐ Heavy-duty battery.
☐ Heavy-duty radiator.

☐ Accent carpeting in red or blue. (Sport Coupe only.)
☐ Color-coordinated floor mats.
☐ Electric clock. (Std. LT.)
☐ Bumper guards.
☐ Door edge guards.
☐ Rear window defogger.
☐ Deluxe seat belts color-keyed to interior. (Not available with black interior.)
☐ Soft-Ray tinted glass. All windows.

☐ Power windows.
☐ Padded vinyl roof cover: black, white, blue, green, cream beige, brown, red, russet, saddle, taupe.
☐ Body side molding.
☐ Bright roof drip molding.
☐ Special instrumentation: tachometer, ammeter and temperature gauge. (Std LT.)
☐ Adjustable driver's seat back.
☐ Front and rear air spoilers.

☐ Comfortilt steering wheel.
☐ Sport suspension (with V8 and F70 or radial tires only.) (Included with Z28.)
☐ Hide-A-Way windshield wipers. (Standard on LT.)
☐ Positraction rear axle. (Included with Z28.)
☐ Trailer-towing package.
☐ Auxiliary Lighting Group: instrument panel, glove and luggage compartments, ashtray and underhood.
☐ Interior Decor/Quiet Sound Group: added sound insulation including full molded hood insulator. (Standard on LT.)
☐ Style Trim Group: bright roof drip molding, body-color door handle accents, bright accents on parking lights, and rear hood molding.
Custom Features your dealer can install.
☐ Audio alarm system.
☐ Battery warmer.
☐ Locking gas cap.
☐ Compass.
☐ Trailer wiring harness.
☐ Trailer hitch.
☐ Highway emergency kit.
☐ Luggage carrier for trunk.
☐ Trunk light.
☐ AM/FM Stereo tape system.
☐ Citizens' Band radio.
☐ Spotlight.
☐ Simulated wire wheel covers.

Availability of Options and Custom Features often depends on model and other equipment selected. Your Chevrolet dealer can answer any questions concerning specific items.

GM
MARK OF EXCELLENCE

In 1975, America was still reeling from the OPEC oil embargo. The national speed limit was decreed to be 55 mph. Gas prices were spiraling upward, when it was available. It was the time of odd/even gas purchase days and 10-gallon limits. People were paranoid about the availability of gasoline and the experts were predicting we would exhaust the earth's petroleum reserves by the end of the 20th century. Economy was the watchword and performance, the antithesis of high mileage, was a villain.

The Z28 went the way of the SS: sacrificed to the god of fuel economy. Even the Rally Sport trim option, though not a performance package, was dropped lest it tempt some lost soul into enjoying his car too much. All that was left for the prospective Camaro buyer was the base Coupe—and the Type LT for those who chose to fly in the face of demand for Spartan economy. It was not a time for people to show openly that they loved their cars. The Rally Sport package did make a comeback at midyear, however.

Increasingly tight emissions regulations forced a new type of equipment on the American public: the catalytic converter. This device extracted a lot of pollutants from the exhaust before dumping it into the atmosphere. But, to protect the converter, only unleaded fuel could be used. This wasn't all bad, because some of the mileage- (and performance-) robbing emission control equipment of previous years could be removed.

Besides the changeover to a catalytic converter, the Camaro underwent a cosmetic change as well. The rear window now wrapped around the sides instead of following the roofline down to the trunk. This greatly improved visibility to the rear quarters and lent an air of openness to the interior.

Engine selection was limited to three on the Sport Coupe and two on the Type LT. A 250 cid six rated at 105 hp was standard on the Coupe, with two-barrel (145 hp) and four-barrel (155 hp) versions of the 350 V-8 optionally available. The two-barrel 350 was standard on the LT, with the four-barrel optional.

Chevrolet went to a lot of trouble trying to convince the public that the Camaro was a small, fuel efficient car, especially considering the investment they had put into convincing them in previous years that it was a performance car. They pointed out the Camaro's "compact" 108-inch wheelbase and claimed that the seating capacity was four adults, which was probably true if the adults in the back seat were under four feet tall.

Midway through the 1975 model year, the Rally Sport option was reintroduced. It offered a visually dramatic and exciting look to the Camaro. The roof, hood and grille were blacked out and a three-color accent strip extended along the edge between the body color and the blacked-out areas. The rocker panels were also blacked out to give the RS a leaner appearance. The RS package could be ordered on either the Sport Coupe or the Type LT.

The Type LT provided a little flair for those who wanted more than basic transportation. Besides the 350 V-8, the package came with full instrumentation, dual sport mirrors and rally wheels, along with the luxury amenities. A wide-range four-speed manual shift transmission was available, as was the D-80 front and rear spoiler option. So, although the times were gray for performance, they weren't totally black. And sales were brisk in spite of the demand for small, economical cars: 145,789 1975 Camaros were produced.

The 1975 Camaro catalogue again followed the similar format to previous editions (see pages 90-92).

THERE'S NO LAW AGAINST DRIVING WITH A SMILE ON YOUR FACE.

You're driving more slowly now, and perhaps you're driving less. But nobody said you had to drive with a frown.

To that principle, and all who applaud it, Chevrolet enthusiastically dedicates the 1975 Camaro.

A beautiful car to drive.

You can see from its shape that Camaro is a *driver's* car. Low profile, wide stance, sloping deck.

And the way it looks is the way it goes.

Camaro responds eagerly when you touch its pedals, stays on track, takes a curve without a lot of lean.

This is the Ninth Annual Edition of Camaro, and although we're probably prejudiced, we think the '75 is the best yet. For two sets of reasons: The things we changed, and the things we left alone.

We'll be talking about both as this book goes along.

Beautifully sensible.

We'd like to remind you that Camaro is and always was a small car.

The wheelbase is a compact 108 inches.

The standard 6-cylinder engine in the standard model is a reasonably economical 250-cubic-inch Six which we've extensively revamped for 1975 to make it more responsive and smoother running.

Thanks to Chevrolet's new Efficiency System, the 1975 Camaro is designed to run leaner (more economically), run cleaner (meet new emission standards) and save you money every mile. It goes farther between recommended

The fine print

Measurements

Wheelbase	108 in.
Length/overall	195.4 in.
Height/loaded	49.1 in.
Width	74.4 in.
Track/front	61.3 in.
Track/front/Type LT	61.6 in.
Track/rear	60.0 in.
Track/rear/Type LT	60.3 in.
Head room/front	37.3 in.
Head room/rear	36.0 in.
Leg room/front	44.1 in.
Leg room/rear	29.6 in.
Shoulder room/front	56.7 in.
Shoulder room/rear	54.4 in.
Hip room/front	52.4 in.
Hip room/front/Type LT	56.2 in.
Hip room/rear	45.8 in.
Curb weight	3532 lbs.
Curb weight/Type LT	3753 lbs.
Trunk capacity/usable	6.4 cu. ft.
Fuel tank capacity	21 gals.
Oil capacity/including filter	4.5 qts.
Coolant capacity/6-cylinder	14 qts.
Coolant capacity/V8	18 qts.
People capacity	4 adults

Occupant Protection

Seat belts with pushbutton buckles for all passenger positions □ Two combination seat and shoulder belts for driver and front passenger (with reminder light and buzzer, inertia reel and starter interlock) □ Two built-in front seat head restraints □ Energy-absorbing steering column □ Passenger-guard door locks □ Safety door latches and hinges □ Folding seat back latches □ Energy-absorbing padded instrument panel and front seat back tops □ Contoured windshield header □ Thick-laminate windshield □ Padded sun visors □ Safety armrests □ Safety steering wheel □ Cargo-guard luggage compartment □ Side-guard door beams □ Contoured roof inner panel.

Accident Prevention

Side marker lights and reflectors (front side marker lights flash with direction signal) □ Parking lights that illuminate with headlights □ Four-way hazard warning flasher □ Back-up lights □ Lane-change feature in direction signal control □ Windshield defrosters, washers and dual-speed wipers □ Wide-view inside day/night mirror (vinyl-edged, shatter-resistant glass and deflecting support) □ Outside rearview mirror □ Dual master cylinder brake system with warning light □ Starter safety switch □ Dual-action safety hood latches.

Anti-Theft

Anti-theft ignition key reminder buzzer □ Anti-theft steering column lock.

Colors

New for 1975: □ Silver □ Light Gray □ Medium Blue □ Bright Blue Metallic □ Midnight Blue Metallic □ Dark Green Metallic □ Sandstone □ Dark Sandstone Metallic □ Light Saddle Metallic □ Medium Orange Metallic. Also offered: □ Antique White □ Medium Green □ Cream Beige □ Bright Yellow □ Light Red □ Dark Red Metallic.
New padded vinyl roof covers available: □ Black or □ White with any exterior color, as well as □ Dark Blue □ Medium Green □ Red □ Dark Red □ Dark Brown □ Sandstone or □ Silver Metallic, depending on exterior color.

Engines

Type	Disp.	Horse-power	Carb. Barrels	Exhaust	Model
Six (1)	250	105	1	Sgl.	Sport Coupe
V8 (2)	350	145	2	Sgl.*	Both
V8 (1)	350	155	4	Sgl.*	Both

*With dual tail pipes.
(1) California Emission Equipment required in California.
(2) Not available in California.

Transmissions

A floor-mounted 3-Speed manual transmission is standard on all Camaros. A floor-mounted 4-Speed manual wide-range is available with the 350-4 barrel V8. Turbo Hydra-matic is available for all models.

Axle Ratios

A new 2.56:1 Highway Axle Ratio is available this year. Four other ratios ranging up to 3.73:1 are offered with various engine/transmission combinations. Standard ratio is 2.73:1. Your dealer will gladly advise as to availability and suitability to your needs.

tune-ups, oil changes, lube jobs and spark plug replacements.

The system includes GM-Specification steel-belted radial tires as standard equipment on both models, High Energy Ignition, catalytic converter and other improvements shown and described on page 5.

Sport Coupe or Type LT.

The important news, however, is that Camaro is what Camaro was: A sensibly sporty compact car that looks like a million and drives like it looks.

We offer two models: The lower priced Sport Coupe and the luxurious Type LT.

And remember this: You don't have to load up a Camaro to enjoy a Camaro. All you have to do is drive it.

© 1974, Chevrolet Motor Division, General Motors Corporation. Many Options and Custom Features are available on all Camaros. Some are illustrated or described in this book.

1975

AVAILABLE:

☐ Sporty center console provides handy storage.

☐ Full wheel covers. (Not avail. on LT.)
☐ Rally wheels. (Std. on LT.)
☐ Choice of radios: AM, AM/FM and AM/FM/Stereo with matched set of speakers. (All factory-installed radios include antenna in windshield.)
☐ Rear seat speaker.
☐ White stripe tires.
☐ Heavy-duty battery.
☐ Heavy-duty radiator.
☐ Power brakes.

☐ Radial-tuned suspension package helps improve ride and handling with Camaro's standard radial ply tires. Includes larger front and added rear stabilizer bars plus special front and rear shock absorbers.

☐ Front and rear spoilers.
☐ Electric clock. (Std. on LT.)
☐ Bumper guards.
☐ Door edge guards.
☐ Soft-Ray tinted glass. All windows.
☐ Power windows.
☐ Color-coordinated floor mats.
☐ Deluxe seat belts, color-keyed to interior. (Not avail. with black interior.)

☐ Padded vinyl roof cover.
☐ Body side molding.
☐ Special instrumentation: tachometer, ammeter, temperature gauge. (Std. on LT.)
☐ Adjustable seat back, driver's side.
☐ Hide-A-Way windshield wipers. (Std. on LT.)
☐ Auxiliary Lighting Group: instrument panel, glove and luggage compartments, ashtray and underhood lights plus "head-lights-on" warning buzzer.

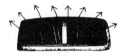

☐ Rear window defogger operates effectively to help clear area of mist.

☐ Sport mirrors. (Std. on LT.)
☐ Dual horns.
☐ Sports Decor Group: sport mirrors, door handle accents, body-color applique below bumpers.
☐ Interior Decor/Quiet Sound Group: additional instrument cluster lighting, wood-grain vinyl instrument accents, added sound insulation including full molded hood insulator. (Std. on LT.)

☐ Power door locks are now available on Camaro for your convenience and security.

☐ Turbine I wheels look like expensive cast aluminum, for an added touch of class.

☐ Style Trim Group: bright roof drip molding, body-color door handle accents, bright accents on parking lights, rear hood molding.
☐ 4-Speed manual transmission.
☐ Turbo Hydra-matic transmission.
☐ Positraction rear axle.
☐ Four-Season air conditioning cools, heats, defrosts, defogs.

☐ Comfortilt steering wheel adjusts to just the right driving angle, raises to ease entry and exit.

Custom Features your dealer can install.

☐ Locking gas cap.
☐ Compass.
☐ Luggage carrier.
☐ Highway emergency kit.
☐ Stereo tape system.
☐ Citizens' Band radio.
☐ Spotlight.
☐ Simulated wire wheel covers.
☐ Audio alarm system.
☐ Battery warmer.
☐ Trailer hitch.

☐ Space-Saver tire takes up less trunk room than regular spare. Comes with compressed gas canister for inflation.

Availability of Options and Custom Features often depends on model and other equipment selected. Your Chevrolet dealer can answer any questions concerning specific items.

All illustrations and specifications contained in this literature are based on the latest product information available at the time of publication approval. The right is reserved to make changes at any time without notice in prices, colors, materials, equipment, specifications and models—and to discontinue models. Chevrolet Motor Division, General Motors Corporation, Detroit, Michigan 48202.

GM
MARK OF EXCELLENCE

Things began to improve in 1976. The harshness of the OPEC oil embargo began to soften and the American public began to regain some of its optimism, though it was cautious optimism.

The Camaro was still limited to two types: the base Sport Coupe and the Type LT. The Rally Sport option could be ordered on either one.

A new engine was offered in 1976: a 305 cid V-8 rated at 140 hp. It was standard on the LT and available on the Coupe. Transmission choices for it were the three-speed manual or automatic. If you wanted a four-speed manual transmission, you had to order the optional 350 V-8, which was now rated at 165 hp. In California, you could get the 350, but only with the automatic transmission. The 250 cid six, still rated at 105 hp, was only available on the Coupe.

The Type LT was still intended to be primarily a luxury-type car, but with a bit of attention to the order sheet, a fair performance car could be engineered. This was how: The LT came with full instrumentation, dual sport mirrors and 14x7 inch rally wheels. On top of that, you could order the 350 V-8, four-speed manual transmission, F-41 handling suspension, and the D-80 front and rear spoiler package. For a little more pizzaz, you could throw in the Rally Sport package.

The RS package came with the blacked-out hood, grille and roof, rimmed by a three-tone, color-keyed pinstripe. The panel between the taillights and the rocker panels was also blacked out, lending to the more aggressive appearance. Although not a Z-28, this package offered reasonable performance and good looks. Obviously the Camaro still attracted a lot of people, because 182,981 1976 Camaros were sold, the third consecutive time that sales exceeded the previous year.

The 1976 Camaro catalogue was a departure from previous years in that it was horizontal, rather than vertical, in format (see pages 94-96).

Camaro Type LT. Shown with available Sport Roof, Custom Styled wheels, white stripe

Camaro Rally Sport. Camaro Sport Coupe shown with available Rally Sport equipm

s. (Shown on cover) Camaro Type LT with available Style Trim Group, white stripe tires.

white stripe tires.

lable on all Camaros. Some are illustrated or described in this book.

Power teams.

Engine	Net HP Rating	Engine* Usage	3-Speed Manual	4-Speed Manual	Turbo Hydra-matic
250 1-bbl. Six (4.1 Litre)	105	Std. N.A. for LT	Std.**	N.A.	Avail.
305 2-bbl. V8 (5.0 Litre)	140	Std.	Std.**	N.A.	Avail.
350 4-bbl. V8 (5.7 Litre)	165	Avail.	N.A.	Avail.**	Avail.

*California Emission Equipment required in California. **Not available in California. N.A.—Not Available

Engines and transmissions.

- New standard 305 V8 engine.
- Quiet hydraulic valve lifters.
- Coolant recovery system helps prevent coolant loss.
- Delcotron generator.
- Single exhaust.
- Turbo Hydra-matic transmission features three forward speed ranges and does the shifting for you automatically. Also, it can be shifted manually when desired.
- Sealed side-terminal energizer-type battery eliminates corrosion

The fine print.

Wheelbase . . . . 108 in.
Length/overall . . . . 195.4 in.
Height/loaded . . . . 49.1 in.
Width . . . . 74.4 in.
Track/front . . . . 61.3 in.
Track/front/Type LT . . . 61.6 in.
Track/rear . . . . 60.0 in.
Track/rear/Type LT . . . . 60.3 in.
Head room/front . . . . 37.3 in.
Head room/rear . . . . 36.0 in.
Leg room/front . . . . 43.9 in.

Leg room/rear . . . . 29.6 in.
Shoulder room/front . . . . 56.7 in.
Shoulder room/rear . . . . . 54.4 in.
Hip room/front . . . . 56.7 in.
Hip room/rear . . . . 47.3 in.
Curb weight/Sport Coupe 3547 lbs.
Curb weight/Type LT . . . 3693 lbs.
Trunk capacity/usable . . . 6.4 cu. ft.
Fuel tank capacity . . . . . . 21 gals.
People capacity . . . . 4 adults

The 1977 model year was the third to debut without the Z28, but fortunately it would be the last. In February of 1977, the Z was reintroduced. Unable to give it the power it had in previous times, thanks to federal emission requirements and fuel economy considerations, the new Z28 placed the emphasis on handling.

New two-color graphics adorned the hood around the non-functional scoop and bold "Z28" decals stood out on the front fenders and rear spoiler. A Z28 emblem was mounted in the grille. Blacked-out grille, headlamp and turn signal housings, window moldings and rocker panels created a leaner, more aggressive appearance. Dual sport mirrors and full instrumentation added to the performance look. But looks weren't all there was to the Z28.

The Z28 engine was still the 350 cid V-8 fitted with the Rochester Quadrajet carburetor. Horsepower was given as 185, not too bad considering the times. Transmission choices were limited to the Borg-Warner four-speed manual with Hurst linkage or the three-speed automatic; California cars were limited to the automatic, period. Also included in the Z28 package were the F-41 suspension, dual exhausts, power brakes (disc front) and GR70x15 radial tires mounted on body-color 15x7 inch Trans Am wheels. The front and rear bumpers were body color with black rubber rub strips.

The rest of the Camaro lineup consisted of the base Sport Coupe and the Type LT, both of which could be ordered with the Rally Sport appearance package. The 250 cid six was now rated at 110 hp and was available only on the Sport Coupe. The 305 V-8 was standard on the Type LT (available on the Sport Coupe) and rated at 145 hp. Available for both was the 170 hp 350 V-8, which you had to order if you wanted a four-speed manual transmission. Because of varying emissions regulations, power train availability began to get very confusing. Only certain rear axle ratios could be fitted to certain engine/transmission combinations, which depended on what part of the country you lived in. Still, the Camaro continued to sell well. For the fourth time in a row, sales were higher than the previous year; 218,854 Camaros were sold in 1977. And considering the late start, it's surprising that 14,349 of them were Z28s.

The 1977 Camaro catalogue returned to the old, traditional vertical format (see pages 100-102). The mid-year Z28 option was immortalized in a black-and-white sheet (see pages 98-99).

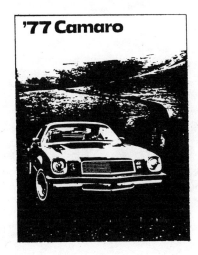

Camaro Z28 Sport Coupe
Back by popular demand

Z28 returns in 1977 with everything you'd expect. It has always been an outstanding road car and '77 is no exception. Once again, a beautiful balance of power, handling equipment and running gear combines to make Z28 a truly precision driving instrument. The picture below illustrates how complete the Z28 equipment package really is.

Performance and handling features

1. 350 C.I.D. 4-bbl. engine
2. Manual transmission
   Heavy-duty Borg-Warner 4-Speed with 2.64 low gear ratio
   Heavy-duty 11-inch clutch
   3.73 performance rear axle ratio
   Automatic transmission (Available—Required in California. Not shown.)
   High shift points (1-2 shift—4900 rpm)
                (2-3 shift—4700 rpm)
   3.42 performance rear axle ratio
3. Low back pressure dual exhaust with resonators
4. Power disc brakes
5. Fast 14:1 ratio power steering for crisp, precise steering
6. High rate front and rear springs
7. Large diameter front stabilizer bar
8. Rear stabilizer bar
9. Shocks with special valving
10. Special suspension bushings and grommets
11. GR70X15 steel belted radial ply white letter tires
12. Special body colored 15" x 7" Z28 wheels
13. Stowaway spare
14. Special instrumentation including tachometer

Trim features

- Black finished grille, headlight bezels, front parking light openings and bezels, windshield and rear window moldings, body sill, rear end panel and taillight bezels
- Front and rear spoilers
- Choice of 7 Camaro Magic-Mirror exterior colors (See reverse side of this page for details)
- Body colored bumpers, door handle inserts and sport mirrors
- Hood decal, wheel opening, body sill and rear spoiler striping color-keyed to body
- Z28 identification on grille, front fenders, rear spoiler, steering wheel and engine air cleaner
- Custom interior available at extra cost (Includes deluxe high-back bucket seats with sidewall trim; special armrests; map pockets in doors; color-keyed instrument panel, steering wheel and column; simulated leather instrument cluster facing)

1977 Z28 CAMARO TRIM SELECTIONS

The Exterior and Interior Color Combinations shown below are
the only combinations that are available.

Seat, Headliner and Door Trim Color	Black	Buckskin	White
Instrument Panel Pad and Carpet Color	Black	Saddle	Black

MODEL	SEAT TYPE			
	Vinyl Bucket	VBB2	VUS2	VWB2
	Custom Vinyl Bucket	XBB2	XUS2	XWB2
1FQ87/Z28				
	Sport Cloth Bucket		JUS2	
	Custom Cloth Bucket		EUS2	

EXTERIOR PAINT COLOR	COLOR L	CODE U				Z28 COLOR SCHEME IDENTIFICATION
Black	19	19	R		R	Package #3
Black	19	19		R		Package #1
Brown (Met)	69	69		R		Package #1
Orange (Met)	78	78		R	R	Package #1
Red, Light	75	75	R		R	Package #3
Silver	13	13	R		R	Package #2
White, Antique	11	11		R		Package #1
White, Antique	11	11	R		R	Package #2
Yellow, Bright	51	51	R		R	Package #4

R—Recommended

	PACKAGE #1	PACKAGE #2	PACKAGE #3	PACKAGE #4
Hood Design	Black Brown Light Gold Yellow-Orange	Black Red Red-Orange Dark Gold	Black Red Red-Orange Dark Gold	Black Yellow-Orange Orange-Yellow Bright Yellow
Body/Spoiler Stripes	Brown Light Gold	Red Red-Orange	Red Red-Orange	Yellow-Orange Orange-Yellow
LETTERING Camaro Z28	Light Gold Lt. Gold/Black/Brown Yellow-Orange	Black Clear/Black/Red/ Red-Orange	Dark Gold Dk. Gold/Black/ Red/Red-Orange	Black Clear/Black/Yellow-Orange/Orange-Yellow

Standard features

There are a lot of them . . . when it's a Camaro! Your Chevrolet dealer can fill you in on any details you might want.

Every '77 Camaro body has these:

• The distinctive Camaro long-hood, short-deck styling with swept-back roof line.
• Hide-A-Way windshield wipers.
• Wraparound taillight units with bright moldings.
• Bright bumpers with protective black rubber rub strips.
• Bright lower body moldings.
• Bright top and side windshield, lower side and full rear window moldings.
• Magic-Mirror acrylic finish in your choice of light blue metallic, dark blue metallic, aqua metallic, medium green metallic, light buckskin, buckskin metallic, brown metallic and orange metallic (all new for '77) plus antique white, silver, black, firethorn metallic, bright yellow and light red.
• Contoured, full foam bucket front seats; bucket-styled, full foam rear seats.
• Soft-rim, vinyl-covered, four-spoke sport steering wheel.
• Built-in heater-defroster system.
• Flow-through power ventilation (starts interior air circulation as soon as ignition is turned on).
• Wall-to-wall, cut-pile, color-keyed carpeting.
• Double-panel steel construction in roof, doors, hood and deck lid.

• Protective inner fenders, front and rear.
• Self-cleaning rocker panels. They permit good air circulation and water drainage to help protect against rust.
• Pre-coated steel used for underbody crossbars and reinforcements for anti-corrosion protection.

These body features are standard on Type LT, available on Sport Coupe:

• Sport mirrors (driver's side remote-controlled).
• Dual horns.
• Rally wheels with bright center caps and trim rings.
• GM-Specification steel-belted radial ply tires.
• Special Instrumentation (includes tachometer, voltmeter, temperature gauge and electric clock).
• Interior Decor/Quiet Sound Group (includes simulated leather trim on instrument cluster, additional instrument lighting, glove compartment light, additional body sound insulation and one-piece hood insulator).

And these body features are exclusive to Type LT:

• Bright grille outline molding.
• Black-finished accent panel under bright lower body molding.
• Brushed-aluminum trim panel between taillights with bright upper and lower moldings.
• Bright trim rings and vertical center bar on parking lights.
• "Type LT" nameplate behind side window and on rear trim panel.
• Special Type LT front bucket seats with deep-contoured backs.
• Special color-coordinated interior trim treatment.

Every '77 Camaro chassis has:

• Variable-ratio power steering.
• Front disc brakes. Fade-resistant and self-adjusting with audible wear sensors that tell when it's time to replace linings.
• Rear drum brakes that are finned to help brakes run cool, resist fade.
• Front stabilizer bar.
• Front coil and rear leaf suspension with springs computer-selected to match car weight as equipped.
• FR78-14 GM-Specification steel-belted radial ply blackwall tires.

Camaro Sport Coupe shown with available Rally Sport Equipment, body side moldings, Style Trim Group, custom-styled wheels, white lettered tires.

Every '77 Camaro engine has:

• High Energy Ignition (a solid-state system that delivers up to 85% hotter spark to the plugs than a conventional system); Carburetor Outside Air Induction (delivers cooler, more dense outside air to the carburetor).
• Hydraulic valve lifters.
• Coolant recovery system to help reduce coolant loss.
• Delcotron generator with solid-state regulator.
• Sealed side-terminal energizer-type battery. Minimizes corrosion buildup on terminals.

Every '77 Camaro offers long recommended service intervals:

Spark plug replacement, up to 22,500 miles; engine oil change, 6 months or 7,500 miles; oil filter replacement, first 7,500 miles, then every 15,000 miles; chassis lubrication, 6 months or 7,500 miles; automatic transmission fluid replacement, 60,000 miles. (Check complete details in Owner's Manual.)

Every '77 Camaro has: For occupant protection.

• Seat belts with pushbutton buckles for all passenger positions.
• Combination seat and inertia reel shoulder belts for driver (with reminder light and buzzer) and right front passenger.
• Energy-absorbing steering column.
• Safety steering wheel.
• Passenger-guard door locks.
• Safety door latches and hinges.
• Folding seat back latches.
• Energy-absorbing padded instrument panel and front seat back tops.

POWER TEAMS

Engine	Power Rating*	Engine Usage	3-Speed Manual Standard (1)	4-Speed Manual Available (1)	Turbo Hydra-matic Available (2)
250-1 barrel Six	110	Standard	2.73† Standard 3.08† Avail. (3)	NA	2.73† Standard 3.08† Avail. (3,4)
305-2 barrel V8	145	Avail. (5,6)	2.73†	NA	2.56†
350-4 barrel V8	170	Avail. (6)	NA	3.08†	2.56† Standard 3.08† Avail. (3,4)

*SAE net (as installed) rating. NA—Not Available. †Axle ratio.
SPECIAL NOTE: California Emission Equipment required for registration in California. In other states, High Altitude Emission Equipment may be required in areas 4,000 feet or more above sea level.
(1) Not available in California or with High Altitude Emission Equipment.
(2) Required in California and with High Altitude Emission Equipment.
(3) Performance ratio.
(4) Included with High Altitude Emission Equipment.
(5) Not available with High Altitude Emission Equipment.
(6) Power brakes required with V8 engines.

• Contoured windshield header.
• Thick-laminate windshield.
• Safety armrests.

For accident prevention.

• Side marker lights and reflectors.
• Parking lamps that illuminate with headlamps.
• Four-way hazard warning flasher.
• Lane-change feature in direction signal control.
• Backup lights.
• Windshield defrosters, washers and dual-speed wipers.
• Wide-view inside, day-night mirror (vinyl-edged, shatter-resistant glass and deflecting support).
• Outside rearview mirror.
• Dual master cylinder brake system with warning light.
• Starter safety switch.
• Dual-action safety hood latch.

For anti-theft.

• Ignition-key reminder buzzer.
• Steering column lock.

DIMENSIONS:

Here's how '77 Camaro sizes up:
Wheelbase	108″
Length	195.4″
Height (loaded)	49.2″
Width	74.4″
Tread, Front	61.3″
(Type LT)	61.6″
Tread, Rear	60.0″
(Type LT)	60.3″
Head room, front	37.3″
Leg room, front	44.1″
Shoulder room, front	56.7″
Hip room, front	52.4″
Head room, rear	36.0″
Leg room, rear	29.6″
Shoulder room, rear	54.4″
Hip room, rear	45.8″
Trunk capacity (usable)	6.4 cu. ft.
Rated fuel tank capacity	21 gals.

Things you can add

Decided whether your '77 Camaro is going to be a Sport Coupe or a Type LT? Now customize it to meet your personal specifications from the list of available equipment shown here. Your salesman can give you more detailed information about each item.

The most popular.

• Center floor console. Includes a concealed storage compartment. Black on Sport Coupe, color-coordinated on Type LT.
• Tinted glass. Highly recommended with air conditioning.
• Sport mirrors. Twin outside rearview mirrors (driver's side is remote controlled) in body or accent color. Standard on Type LT.
• Air conditioning, Four-Season. Includes heavy-duty radiator (on six-cylinder models) and 61-amp Delcotron generator.
• Consider the Delco sound systems produced to General Motors and Chevrolet quality standards. Only genuine Delco radios carry the Delco-GM trademark. Factory-installed windshield antenna included. Your choice of: pushbutton AM radio (single speaker), pushbutton AM/FM stereo or monaural radio (dual speakers), AM radio with 8-track stereo tape system (dual speakers), AM/FM stereo radio with 8-track stereo tape system (dual speakers). Also auxiliary rear seat speaker (not available with stereo or tape systems).
• Body side bright molding. Helps protect against carelessly opened doors of parallel parkers.
• Rally wheels (std. on Type LT). Special wheels with bright center hubs and trim rings.
• Style Trim Group. Includes bright moldings for roof drip, side windows, hood edge and belt line. Also color-insert door handles and bright-accented parking lights.

The Rally Sport.

A very dramatic appearance package available for either the Sport Coupe or the Type LT. Features special contrasting paint areas (in your choice of low-gloss black or, new-for-'77, gray metallic, dark blue metallic or buckskin metallic) on forward portion of roof, rear end panel and license opening, around side windows, on upper portion of doors, top surface of front fenders, hood, header panel and on dual sport mirrors (included in Rally Sport Equipment package). Grille and lower body area are black. A distinctive tri-color striping separates the contrasting color from the body color in appropriate areas. Package also includes bright-edged headlight bezels, Rally wheels (both std. on Type LT) and "Rally Sport" decals on deck lid and front fenders. Ask about exterior colors available with the package.

Other available appearance equipment.

• Vinyl sport roof cover. Extends across front part of roof for distinctive look.
• Deluxe color-keyed seat belts and front seat shoulder belts (not available with black or white/black interior).
• Floor mats, front and rear, color-keyed.
• Steel-belted radial ply blackwall tires (std. on Type LT).
• White stripe or white lettered tires.
• Full wheel covers (not available with Rally wheels).
• Custom-styled urethane/steel wheels (available only with steel-belted radial ply tires).

Other available comfort and convenience equipment.

• Comfortilt steering wheel. Adjusts to any of six steering wheel angles you desire, tilts up and out of the way for easy entrance and exit.
• Two-position adjustable driver's seat back provides alternate seat-back angle. Natural comfort companion to the Comfortilt steering wheel.
• Power windows. Control buttons under your fingertips on the center floor console that's required with power windows.
• Intermittent windshield wipers. Wipers can be adjusted to make one sweep, then pause before making next sweep.
• Cruise-Master speed control. Available on automatic transmission-equipped Camaros only (not available on Six in California). Automatically maintains speed selected by the driver. Stepping on brake automatically disengages control.

• Rear window defogger. Powerful forced-air design quickly clears rear window frost or fog.
• Interior Decor/Quiet Sound Group (std. on Type LT). Provides added instrument lighting, simulated leather on instrument cluster, additional body insulation and hood insulator.
• Special Instrumentation (std. on Type LT). Adds a tachometer, voltmeter, temperature gauge and electric clock to standard panel. Electric clock may be ordered separately.
• Auxiliary Lighting Group. Adds underhood, ashtray and courtesy lights, glovebox light (std. on Type LT), headlight reminder buzzer.
• Power door locks.
• Bumper guards, front and rear.
• Door edge guard moldings.

Additional mechanical & performance available equipment.

• Spoilers, front and rear.
• Sport suspension. Includes larger front and added rear stabilizer bars, "high effort feel" power steering and shock absorber valving calibrated for a somewhat firmer ride. Requires steel-belted radial ply tires on Sport Coupe.
• Heavy-duty battery.
• Positraction. For added rear wheel traction.
• Dual horns (std. on Type LT).
• Radiator, heavy-duty. Included with air conditioning on six-cylinder models.
• Stowaway spare. Increases usable trunk space.
• Trailering equipment (ask your salesman for details).

The lines of the 1978 Camaros were smoothed out a bit by using molded-in bumpers at the front and rear. The one-piece front included the grille surround, turn signal and headlight housings and just a hint of an air dam on the bottom. Also new that year were larger, three-segment taillights, with red lenses on the outside that wrapped around to include side marker lights, amber turn signal lenses in the center part and clear backup light lenses on the inner portion.

The Z28 graphics were revised for 1978. On the hood, two-color stripes flared out around the non-functional scoop, with matching narrow stripes outlining the "intake" area. The Z28 emblem on the grille and the decals on the front fenders, carried that same two colors in a 3-D effect. A matching two-color pinstripe accented the lower body line, arcing over the wheel well lips, wrapping around the front on the air dam lip and separating the body color from the blacked-out rocker panels. Also blacked out were the grille, headlight and turn signal recesses, hood scoop "intake" area, all window moldings and the panel between the taillights. A non-functional five-slot louver was mounted on each front fender, above the body crease behind the wheel well.

Along with the graphics, the Z28 package included the 350 V-8, now rated at 170 hp in 49-state tune, 160 in California. A four-speed manual transmission was available on 49-state cars, but the optional automatic was all that could be had on California versions. All Z28s came with the F-41 suspension, dual exhausts and resonators, 15x7 inch body-color Trans Am wheels fitted with GR70x15 radial tires, power front disc brakes, full instrumentation and dual mirrors. The rear spoiler was now also included as part of the package. The only rear axle ratios available were 3.73:1 for four-speed equipped models and 3.42:1 for automatics. Vaned aluminum wheels were offered as an option for the 1978 Z28 and proved to be quite popular.

The rest of the 1978 Camaro lineup consisted of the Sport Coupe and Type LT, either of which could be ordered with the Z28 or Rally Sport package, but not both. The Rally Sport package again featured a blacked-out roof, hood and headlight/grille area trimmed by a three-tone, color-keyed pinstripe. The grille, window moldings, rocker panels and panel between the taillight lenses were also blacked out, with the headlight and front turn signal recesses chrome accented.

For the fifth straight time, Camaro sales topped the previous year. A total of 272,631 1978 Camaros were sold. Of this total, 54,907 were Z28s.

The 1978 Camaro catalogue followed the familiar format (see pages 104-108). There was no Z28 brochure.

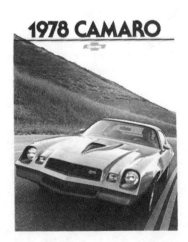

1978 CAMARO

CAMARO Z28

It'll put butterflies in your stomach, a lump in your throat and a smile on your face.

It's exciting, it's virile, it's a legend. Owning and driving a Z28 is a rare experience enjoyed most by those who enjoy driving the most.

Exclusive to Z28 are the louvers in the front fenders and the simulated air induction scoop in the hood. Beneath the sloping hood you'll find a 350 Cu. In. V8 with four-barrel carburetion.

A 4-Speed close-ratio manual transmission and special 3.73* performance ratio rear axle (3.42 also available with automatic transmission—required

350 Cu. In. V8   Dual resonator/tailpipe   Special springs   15" body-color wheels   Special shocks / Front stabilizer   Wh

2.

in California) get the power to the white lettered GR70-15 steel-belted radials mounted on special Z28 body-colored seven-inch wheels. A special Sport suspension helps keep you in touch with the road.

The cockpit features Special Instrumentation, including: tachometer, voltmeter, temperature gage and electric clock. You also get a space-saving Stowaway spare tire.

Also included: Z28 identification and accent striping, a rear spoiler, dual sport mirrors (driver's side remote controlled) and black-finished grille and reveal moldings around the windshield and rear window, black-finished headlight and parking light bezels.

The Z28 is available in the following body colors: white, silver metallic, black, bright blue metallic, dark blue-green metallic, bright yellow, camel metallic, dark camel metallic, red, carmine metallic and yellow-orange. There are 9 accent stripe combinations available.

*Except in California.

Camaro Z28 with available aluminum wheels (shown above and on cover).

3

105

CAMARO
RALLY SPORT

Driving excitement, and then some.

Camaro is our way of helping you escape from what too often becomes the routine task of driving. When you take the wheel of a Camaro, you take command—because Camaro is, and always has been, a driver's car. No matter what kind of driving you do, one

Camaro Rally Sport with available removable glass roof panels, white stripe tires and tinted glass.

thing's for sure. You won't get bored in the driver's seat of a Camaro.

New front and rear styling in soft, resilient urethane adds even more flair to Camaro's great shape and stance.

The action starts with Camaro Rally Sport Coupe featured below with the new removable glass roof panels (slightly reduce head room) available on all Camaros. A Type LT Rally Sport Coupe model is also available this year.

Rally Sport models feature black finish on the hood and portions of the front fenders and top. Five tri-tone accent stripes are available, color-keyed to the interior color and your choice of the following body colors: white, silver, light blue metallic, bright yellow, camel metallic and red. Other features include Rally Sport identification, rear spoiler, Rally wheels, dual sport mirrors and black-finished grille and headlight bezels.

Both the Camaro Type LT Coupe and the Camaro Sport Coupe are available with Rally Sport equipment as model options.

CAMARO EFFICIENCY...
AND OTHER STANDARDS

Standard features and specifications:

1. Coolant recovery system to help reduce coolant loss.
2. Delco Freedom battery that never needs water.
3. Hide-A-Way windshield wipers.
4. Flow-through ventilation.
5. Double-panel steel construction in roof, doors, hood and deck lid.
6. Protective inner fenders, front and rear.
7. Power steering.
8. Front disc brakes. Fade-resistant and self-adjusting with audible wear sensors that tell when it's time to replace pad.
9. Rear drum brakes that are finned to help brakes run cool, resist fade.
10. Front stabilizer bar.
11. Contoured, full-foam bucket seats; bucket-styled full-foam back seats.
12. Wall-to-wall, cut-pile, color-keyed carpeting.

Also standard:

- Delcotron generator with built-in solid-state regulator.
- New integral coil distributor cap helps protect coil from heat and moisture.
- New fuel vapor canister captures vapors from the carburetor as well as the fuel tank after engine shutdown for improved vapor recovery and emission control.
- Body by Fisher.

- New front styling in resilient urethane with energy-absorbing soft fascia, body-colored front bumper system.
- New rear styling with tri-colored taillights and soft, body-colored, energy-absorbing bumper system..
- Bright lower body moldings.
- All-vinyl interiors in black, green, camel and carmine.
- All-vinyl 2-tone interior comes with white bucket seats, headliner and door trim; instrument panel, carpet, cowl side panels and rear shelf in your choice of black, blue, green, carmine or saffron.
- Bright windshield, lower side and full rear window moldings (except Z28).
- Magic-Mirror acrylic finish in your choice of bright blue metallic, dark blue-green metallic, camel metallic, saffron metallic, dark camel metallic and carmine metallic (all new for '78), plus white, silver, black, light blue, bright yellow and light red.
- Soft-rim, vinyl-covered, four-spoke sport steering wheel.
- Built-in heater-defroster system.
- Self-cleaning rocker panels. They are vented to permit good air circulation and water drainage which helps protect against rust.
- Precoated steel used for underbody crossbars and reinforcements aids in corrosion resistance.
- Front coil and rear leaf suspension with springs computer-selected to match car weight as equipped.
- FR78-14 GM Specification steel-belted radial ply blackwall tires.

'78 Camaro dimensions:

Wheelbase	108.0"
Length	197.6"
Height (loaded)	49.2"
Width	74.4"
Tread, front	61.3"
(Type LT)	61.6"
Tread, rear	60.0"
(Type LT)	60.3"
Head room, front	37.3"
Leg room, front	44.1"
Shoulder room, front	56.7"
Hip room, front	52.4"
Head room, rear	36.0"
Leg room, rear	29.6"
Shoulder room, rear	54.4"
Hip room, rear	45.8"
Trunk capacity (usable)	6.3 cu. ft.
Rated fuel tank capacity	21 gals.

1978 Camaro power teams: All States Except California

Engines	Power Rating†	Engine Availability Type LT & Sport Coupe	Z28	3-Speed Manual (STD.)	4-Speed Manual	4-Speed Close-Ratio Manual††	Automatic Below 4,000 Ft.	Automatic 4,000 Ft. and Above
250 Cu. In. L6	110	STD.	NA	2.73	NA	NA	2.73	NA
305 Cu. In. V8	145	AVAIL.	NA	NA	3.08	NA	2.41	NA
350 Cu. In. V8	170/160▲	AVAIL.	STD.	NA	3.08	3.73	2.41*/3.42**	3.08/3.42**

California Only

Engines	Power Rating†	Engine Availability Type LT & Sport Coupe	Z28	3-Speed Manual (STD.)	4-Speed Manual	4-Speed Close-Ratio Manual††	Automatic Below 4,000 Ft.	Automatic 4,000 Ft. and Above
250 Cu. In. L6	90	STD.	NA	NA	NA	NA	2.73	NA
305 Cu. In. V8	135	AVAIL.	NA	NA	NA	NA	2.41	NA
350 Cu. In. V8	160	AVAIL.	STD.	NA	NA	NA	2.41*/3.42**	NA

†S.A.E. net horsepower as installed.   *3.08 Performance Ratio available.   **Z28 only.
▲Rating with High Altitude Emission Equipment.   ††4-Speed Close-Ratio Manual Z28 only.
STD.—Standard.   NA—Not Available.

SPECIAL NOTE: California Emission Equipment required for registration in California. In other states, High Altitude Emission Equipment may be required in areas 4,000 feet or more above sea level.

The Z28 got a bolder, more aggressive look in 1979 with the addition of a deep front air dam that wrapped around the front and formed fender flares blending into the leading edge of the wheel wells. Bold two-color stripes proclaimed "Z28" at the rear of the doors, streaked forward onto the front fenders, then narrowed and dipped to wrap around the nose on the lower front lip of the air dam. A matching two-color stripe wrapped over the tail-lights and center panel, underneath the spoiler. Centered in the stripe were the characters "Z28." Instead of an emblem on the grille, a matching two-color decal was affixed to the upper left of the grille surround. Stripes in the same two colors flared out around the non-functional hood scoop, with a matching pinstripe outlining the blacked-out "intake" area. Non-functional five-slot louvers were mounted on the front fenders.

The Z28 package still included the F-41 suspension, power front disc brakes, dual sport mirrors, full instrumentation, four-speed manual transmission or optional automatic (required in California), dual exhausts, rear spoiler and front air dam. The 350 cid Z28 engine was rated at 175 hp in 49-state trim and 170 for California. Rear axle ratios were limited to 3.73:1 for manual-transmissioned Zs, 3.42:1 for automatics. Tires were GR70x15 radials mounted on body-color 15x7 inch Trans Am rims; vaned aluminum wheels were again offered as an option.

The Type LT was discontinued in 1979, replaced by the Berlinetta, a smooth-riding upscale Camaro with a true Grand Touring feel. The Rally Sport became a separate model as opposed to being a trim package, although the big feature was still the blacked-out hood, nose and roof with three-tone, color-keyed pinstripe outline, plus the blacked-out rocker panels and rear panel. The Sport Coupe remained the entry-level Camaro.

The standard engine for all non-Z28 models was the 250 cid six, rated at 115 hp, which came with the three-speed manual transmission but could be teamed with the automatic. The 305 cid (130 hp) and 350 cid (170 hp) V-8s were optional, but had to be teamed with either the wide-range four-speed manual or automatic transmission, except in California. There, the only transmission ofered for any engine was the automatic. Horsepower ratings for California engines were 90 for the six, 125 for the 305 and 165 for the non-Z28 350.

Once again, sales topped the previous year, further justifying the decision to continue making them back in 1971. A total of 282,571 1979 Camaros were made, and an impressive 84,877 of them were Z28s.

The 1979 Camaro catalogue was similar to that of previous years (see pages 110-120).

Camaro

1979

Camaro.
The Hugger.

Ever since they first got together,
Camaros and America's roads have been
very close friends.
 Wherever you go you see the two of
them, running together, enjoying this land
together. Roads and road cars, meant for
each other.
 Led by the Z28, a truly impressive
road car.

Through twelve years of road-
hugging, the Camaro suspension has
been continually refined. A front stabilizer
is standard equipment. So's power
steering.
 The wheels are widespread with
standard steel-belted radial ply tires.
 And this year there's a bright new
Camaro personality for you to choose

Shown on cover:
Camaro Z28 in white, Rally Sport in bright yellow and black, Berlinetta in dark blue metallic and Sport Coupe in red

Camaro Berlinetta with available AM/FM radio, rear window defogger, tinted glass and air conditioning.

from. The new Camaro Berlinetta.
A new level of extraordinary road looks
and a boulevard ride. The suspension is
engineered for relaxing comfort. The
richly upholstered bucket seats are
distinctly Berlinetta

A new Chevrolet Camaro and a
favorite road of yours: Why not get them
together

A word about this catalog:
*We have tried to make this catalog as
comprehensive and factual as possible
And we hope you find it helpful. However,
since the time of printing, some of the
information you'll find here may have
been updated. Also, some of the
equipment shown or described
throughout this brochure is available at*

*extra cost. Your dealer has details and
before ordering, you should ask him to
bring you up to date*

The right is reserved to make changes at any time
without notice in prices, colors, materials, equipment
specifications and models, and to discontinue models
Check with your Chevrolet dealer for complete
information.

5.7 Litre 4-Bbl. V8 (350 Cu. In.).   Dual resonators/tailpipes.   Special springs.   15" x 7" body-color wheels.   Special shocks/front and rear stabilizers.

Camaro Z28 shown in white. Features shown above are standard on Z28.

Camaro Z28

The Z28 makes waves. It's a car that goes from one point to another with the kind of sleek road authority that causes talk and creates legends.

The kind that comes from years of fussy automotive research and continually refined Camaro engineering. From the special Z28 Sport suspension, performance rear axle, power brakes and

from a precision-built 4-Speed close-ratio manual transmission. (Automatic required in California.)

And from the burly 5.7 Litre 4-Bbl. V8 that lives harnessed under that gently sloping hood.

Inside the Z28 cockpit, you lean back and preside over a bank of carefully placed instruments. It's a vigilant

ite-lettered tires supplied   Special Instrumentation.   Front disc brakes.   3.73 rear axle.   Four-Speed close-ratio manual transmission
arious manufacturers.   (automatic transmission required in California).

nformation center that continuously eeds you vital performance readouts. It ncludes a tachometer, voltmeter, emperature gage and electric clock astefully set in black chrome.

And a special large-rim steering wheel eips put all the Z28 motion and grace ight in the palm of your hand.

Outside, the Z28 is not at all shy about proclaiming its remarkable personality. It's a bold statement that starts with white lettered, steel-belted radial ply tires on color-keyed wheels. And continues with a simulated air induction scoop, simulated air louvers in the front fenders, a rear spoiler and dual sport mirrors. And this year there's a new low-slung air dam and new front wheel opening flares.

To complete the image of a most impressive road car, there are the Z28 identification, accent striping, distinctive black-finished grille, reveal moldings around the windshield and rear window, and striking black-finished headlight and parking light frames.

And it all comes to life with the turn of a little key.

Camaro Berlinetta shown in dark blue metallic with available aluminum wheels and white lettered tires which are supplied by various manufacturers

Camaro Berlinetta

We've brought into this world a Camaro that has layer upon layer of sumptuous comfort and ease.

Berlinetta. It's the bold signature of an extraordinary new Camaro.

First and foremost, Berlinetta has the same engineering features most other Camaros are born with. Road-hugging, finely tuned suspension. An aggressive 4.1 Litre 1-Bbl. L6 (250 Cu. In.) engine. The streamlined body that parts the air with nimble ease.

But beyond that, Berlinetta has been given a whole new level of good looks and riding comfort. A deluxe insulating package helps keep out wind and road noise. Engine mounts have been custom tuned. The shocks revalved. Front spring

isolators and large body mounts smooth
rough roads and help provide a lush,
balanced ride.

Plus, you'll find newly designed front
bucket seats, with custom-tailored fabrics
and cushioned comfort that seems
fathoms deep. There's a bright-accented
Special Instrumentation panel, too, with
tachometer, voltmeter, temperature gage

and electric clock.

Outside, there's a bright new
Berlinetta grille to let the world know that
something remarkable is coming on
through. Plus dual pin stripes,
color-keyed custom styled wheels, white
stripe tires, dramatic black-painted rocker
panels and new Berlinetta identification
on front end, trunk lid and rear roof panels.

Camaro Rally Sport shown in bright yellow and black with available removable glass roof panels. tinted glass. white-stripe tires and Custom interior.

Camaro Sport Coupe shown in silver with available full wheel covers. sport mirrors. white-stripe tires and bright roof drip moldings

Camaro
Rally Sport

With that unmistakable blackout grille, distinctive body paint treatment and stylish rear spoiler, the Rally Sport is the very spirit of road magic from beginning to end. Styling and performance are equals here. Two parts of the same winning personality.

First off, on the style side, there's that special exterior color pattern. The hood and forward part of the roof are painted one of three colors—dark blue, black or camel—that's keyed to the body color you choose. It's a bold, stunning effect that shows off Camaro's naturally sleek skin and structure.

Additional styled highlights include black body sill, sport mirrors, tri-color striping and color-keyed Rally wheels.

The 4.1 Litre L6 engine is standard. And the Rally Sport hugs the road with a set of steel-belted radial ply tires, front stabilizer, special shock absorbers and power steering.

Also included are the Rally Sport identification and bright-finished parking and headlight bezels.

And the good times. They also come standard in a Rally Sport.

Camaro
Sport Coupe

Where Camaro fun begins.

If movement is pleasure, then the Sport Coupe was made for pleasure. From its aerodynamically sleek lines to its standard 4.1 Litre L6 (250 Cu. In.) engine, it is a car that loves to move.

So that you can move in comfort, there's an exciting, plush Camaro interior with full-foam bucket seats and cut-pile carpeting.

To make it responsive, exciting and special, there's Camaro's road-balanced suspension with front stabilizer bar, power steering and steel-belted radial ply tires.

And for a little extra dash and style, you get bright body sill moldings.

The Camaro Sport Coupe. Both affordable and fun.

Camaro standard features

1. Delco Freedom battery. Never needs refilling. Sealed side terminals help resist corrosion.

2. Concealed windshield wipers. Disappear when wipers are switched off. Helps preserve the clean, sculptured lines of hood and windshield.

3. Coolant recovery system. Helps prevent loss of coolant.

4. Front disc/rear drum brakes. A self-adjusting system. Fade-resistant front disc brakes have audible wear sensors to let you know when to replace linings.

5. Front coil and rear leaf suspension. With springs computer-selected to match car weight as equipped.

6. Power steering. Puts you in touch with the road with little effort.

7. Inner fenders. Inner shield on front and rear fenders helps provide road splash protection.

8. Double-wall construction. Provides two layers of steel in doors, roof, hood and deck lid.

9. High Energy Ignition. A solid-state system that eliminates points and ignition condenser, yet delivers a high-voltage spark that helps extend time between recommended tune-ups.

10. Front stabilizer bar. Helps reduce body lean during sharp turns.

11. Contoured, full-foam front bucket seats. Plus bucket-styled full-foam back seats.

12. Wall-to-wall carpeting. Lush, cut-pile, color-keyed carpeting.

13. Steel-belted radial ply tires. Offer lower rolling resistance than conventional bias ply tires and impressive traction.

14. Flow-through ventilation system. Outside air flows from outlets in the instrument panel, over front seat to back seat under all driving conditions.

15. Visible ball joint wear indicators. Located on front suspension lower control arms for visual check of ball joint wear.

MORE STANDARDS

Delcotron generator with built-in solid-state regulator • Integral coil distributor cap helps protect coil from heat and moisture • Fuel vapor canister captures vapors from the carburetor as well as the fuel tank after engine shutdown for improved vapor recovery and emission control • Body by Fisher • Front and rear styling in resilient urethane with energy-absorbing soft fascia, body-colored front and rear bumper system • Bright windshield and full rear window reveal moldings (except Z28) • New improved Exhaust Gas Recirculation (EGR) and cold trapped spark control system for 5.0 and 5.7 Litre V8 engines (49 states application) contribute to good drivability. • New instrument panel pad and cluster bezel styling • Soft-rim, vinyl-covered four-spoke sport steering wheel • Built-in heater-defroster system • Ventilated rocker panels are designed to permit good air circulation and water drainage which helps protect against rust • Precoated steel used for underbody crossbars and reinforcement aids in corrosion resistance • Catalytic converter • Carburetor outside air intake.

For features standard to Berlinetta, Z28 and Rally Sport, see pages 4 through 9.

DIMENSIONS (inches)

EXTERIOR	Berlinetta	All Models Except Berlinetta
Wheelbase	108.0	108.0
Length (overall)	197.6	197.6
Width (overall)	74.5	74.5
Height (loaded)	49.2	49.2
Tread-Front	61.6	61.3
Tread-Rear	60.3	60.0

INTERIOR		
Head Room-Front	37.2	37.2
Head Room-Rear	36.0	36.0
Leg Room-Front	43.9	43.9
Leg Room-Rear	28.4	28.4
Hip Room-Front	55.3	55.3
Hip Room-Rear	46.3	46.3
Shoulder Room-Front	56.7	56.7
Shoulder Room-Rear	54.4	54.4
Usable Luggage Capacity (cu. ft.)	6.4*	6.4*

*7.2 cu. ft. with available Stowaway spare tire.

A WORD ABOUT ENGINES

The Chevrolets shown in this catalog are equipped with GM-built engines produced by various divisions. Please refer to the Camaro Power Teams Chart on this page and see your dealer for details.

ENGINE SELECTION

4.1 LITRE L6

Engine is standard on all models except the Z28. It features a fully counter-weighted, seven-main-bearing crankshaft for smoothness and strength. Hydraulic valve lifters help provide a smooth and quiet flow of power. It's an engine that delivers the kind of performance you need for today's kind of driving.

5.0 LITRE V8

This available engine features short-stroke valve-in-head design and downdraft carburetor which help provide good engine performance at all speed ranges. You also get full jacket cylinder cooling, a precision-balanced crankshaft and hydraulic valve lifters.

5.7 LITRE V8

A rugged available powerplant with impressive low-speed torque for around town cruising, but also responsive on the highway and well-suited for hilly driving, big loads or trailering.

CAMARO POWER TEAMS

Engine	Ordering Code	Power Rating*	Displacement (cubic inches)	Engine Availability		Transmission Availability			
				All Models Except Z28	Z28 Only	Three-Speed Manual (1)	Four-Speed Manual (1)	Four-Speed Close-Ratio Manual (1)	Auto-matic (2)
ALL STATES EXCEPT CALIFORNIA									
4.1 Litre 1-Bbl. L6 (A)	L22	115	250	Std.	NA	Std.	NA	NA	EC
5.0 Litre 2-Bbl. V8 (B)	LG3	130	305	EC (3)	NA	NA	EC	NA	EC
5.7 Litre 4-Bbl. V8 (B)	LM1	170	350	EC (3)	NA	NA	EC	NA	EC
5.7 Litre 4-Bbl. V8 (B)	LM1	175	350	NA	Std.	NA	NA	Std.	EC
ALL STATES EXCEPT CALIFORNIA (with High Altitude Emission Equipment)									
5.7 Litre 4-Bbl. V8 (B)	LM1	165	350	EC (3)	NA	NA	NA	NA	EC
CALIFORNIA ONLY (with California Emission Requirements)									
4.1 Litre 1-Bbl. L6 (A)	L22	90	250	Std.	NA	NA	NA	NA	EC
5.0 Litre 2-Bbl. V8 (B)	LG3	125	305	EC (3)	NA	NA	NA	NA	EC
5.7 Litre 4-Bbl. V8 (B)	LM1	165	350	EC (3)	NA	NA	NA	NA	EC
5.7 Litre 4-Bbl. V8 (B)	LM1	170	350	NA	Std.	NA	NA	NA	EC

*S.A.E. net horsepower as installed.   Std.—Standard.   NA—Not Available.   EC—Available at extra cost.
(1) With floor-mounted shift control.   (2) Floor console (RPO D55) required.   (3) Power brakes (RPO J50) required.

(A) PRODUCED BY GM—CHEVROLET MOTOR DIVISION.
(B) PRODUCED BY GM—CHEVROLET MOTOR DIVISION AND GM OF CANADA.

LONG RECOMMENDED SERVICE INTERVALS

(Under normal driving conditions with standard 4.1 Litre 1-Bbl. L6 (250 Cu. In.) engine)

Engine Oil . . . . .12 months or 7,500 miles

Oil Filter . . . . .First 7,500 miles; every 15,000 thereafter

Spark Plugs . . . . .45,000 miles in 49 states; 30,000 miles in California*

Chassis Lubrication . . . . . . .12 months or 7,500 miles

Automatic Transmission Fluid Change . . . . .Every 100,000 miles

*All V8 engines: 22,500 miles.

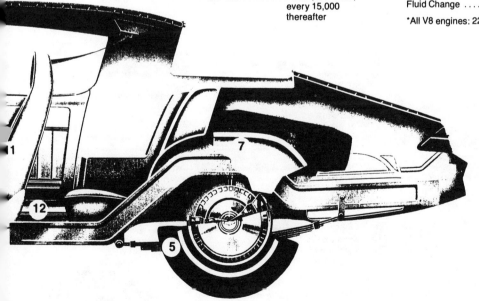

Reasons to buy Camaro

- **Exciting, sporty, streamlined appearance.**
- **Traditionally high resale value.**
- **Spirited performance.**
- **Fun to drive with impressive roadability.**
- **Wide range of engines available.**

- **Quality engineered and designed for value.**
  - —**Stub frame construction with six isolating body mounts.**
  - —**Extensive use of anti-corrosion treatments and materials.**
  - —**Long recommended service intervals.**

BUILD YOUR OWN CAMARO
(See your dealer for current ordering information.)

MODELS

☐ Berlinetta   ☐ Z28   ☐ Rally Sport   ☐ Sport Coupe

COLORS (See chart on page 10 for color availabilities and combinations.)

Exterior color_____   Second color (on Rally Sport only)_____   Sport Roof color_____
Interior color_____   Upholstery (cloth or vinyl)_____

ENGINES (See chart on page 13 for engine/transmission availability.)

☐ 4.1 Litre 1-Bbl. L6 (250 Cu. In.)—Std.   ☐ 5.0 Litre 2-Bbl. V8 (305 Cu. In.)—Avail.   ☐ 5.7 Litre 4-Bbl. V8 (350 Cu. In.)—Avail.

TRANSMISSIONS

☐ Automatic (Avail.)*   ☐ Three-Speed manual (Std.)†   ☐ Four-Speed manual (Avail.)†   ☐ Four-Speed manual close ratio (Std.)**†

AVAILABLE OPTIONS

☐ Power windows
☐ Air conditioning
☐ Deluxe color-keyed seat and shoulder belts
☐ Power brakes
☐ Electric clock
☐ Comfortilt steering wheel
☐ Console
☐ Automatic Speed Control
☐ Power door lock system
☐ Electric rear window defogger
☐ Tinted glass
☐ Auxiliary lighting
☐ Special Instrumentation (Includes electric clock, tachometer, voltmeter and engine temperature gages)
☐ Interior Decor/Quiet Sound Group
☐ Intermittent windshield wiper system
☐ Custom interior

MOLDINGS AND TRIM
☐ Door edge guards
☐ Roof drip moldings
☐ Body side moldings
☐ Rear spoiler
☐ Style Trim Group

☐ Sport Roof (vinyl over front portion of roof)

SOUND EQUIPMENT
☐ AM radio
☐ AM/FM radio
☐ AM/FM/Citizens Band radio with power antenna
☐ AM/FM stereo/Citizens Band radio with power antenna
☐ AM/FM stereo radio
☐ AM radio with 8-track stereo tape
☐ AM/FM stereo radio with 8-track stereo tape
☐ AM/FM stereo radio with stereo cassette tape
☐ AM/FM stereo radio with digital clock display
☐ Rear seat speaker
☐ Windshield antenna
☐ Power antenna

WHEELS AND WHEEL COVERS
☐ Aluminum wheels
☐ Full wheel covers
☐ Color-keyed Rally wheels

☐ Custom styled wheels

TIRES
☐ E78-14 bias-belted ply blackwall
☐ E78-14 bias-belted ply white stripe
☐ FR78-14 steel-belted radial ply blackwall tires
☐ FR78-14 steel-belted radial ply white stripe
☐ FR78-14 steel-belted radial ply white lettered

MISCELLANEOUS
☐ Removable glass roof panels
☐ Performance axle ratio
☐ High altitude emission equipment
☐ Color-keyed floor mats front and rear
☐ Dual horns
☐ Sport mirrors, LH remote and RH manual
☐ Heavy-duty radiator
☐ Adjustable driver's seat back
☐ Stowaway spare tire
☐ Sport suspension
☐ Heavy-duty battery
☐ Limited slip differential

*Required in California.
**Standard with Z28 only.
†Not available in California or with High Altitude Emission Equipment.

Chevrolet

For the first time, two different engines were used in the Z28. In order to comply with tougher California emission requirements, Chevrolet used the 305 cid (5-liter) V-8 teamed with the automatic transmission in that state. The 350 cid (5.7 liter) V-8 remained the engine for the 49-state version of the Z, teamed with a four-speed manual or automatic transmission. The California engine was rated at 165 hp, the 49-state model at 190. The increased power in the 49-state edition was due to a new solenoid-activated cold air intake through the now-functional hood scoop.

With the extra power came a new look, more aggressive than in previous years. The simulated louvers on the front fenders were replaced by functional single-port heat exhausts like the ones used on Firebird Trans Ams. The side stripes were now a fluorescent tricolor, with the Z, 2 and 8 standing the full height of the stripes where they ended at the rear of the doors. The stripes ran forward, narrowing as they dipped down on the front fender flares to run along the lower front lip of the deep air dam. The "Z28" emblems in the grille and on the fuel filler door carried the same three colors as the stripes. A matching tricolor pinstripe ran along the top outside edge of the hood scoop and on each side of it, in big block letters, were the words "AIR INDUCTION." Another tricolor pinstripe ran across the back between the taillights and the spoiler. Blackout accents were used on all window moldings,

the headlamp and turn signal recesses, the rocker panels and the grille, which now featured wide-spaced horizontal bars instead of the previous rectangular grid.

The Z28 package also included the F-41 suspension, dual exhausts with resonators, full instrumentation, and power front disc brakes. Rear axle ratios were 3.08:1 for four-speed equipped models and 3.42:1 for automatics.

Other Camaro choices for 1980 consisted of the Berlinetta, the Rally Sport and the base Sport Coupe. Available engines changed for 1980; the standard engine for non-Z28s was the new 3.8 liter V-6, rated at 115 hp (110 in California). This was teamed with the three-speed manual transmission, but an automatic could be ordered (required in California). A 4.4 liter V-8 rated at 120 hp was available in the 49-state models; automatic transmission was required. The 5.0 liter (305 cid) V-8 was available and rated at 155 hp in all 50 states. A four-speed manual transmission was available in 49-state trim, but the optional automatic was required in California.

Although still popular, sales of the Camaro started to dip in 1981. Only 152,005 were sold, of which 45,137 were Z28s.

The 1980 Camaro catalogue, in the long-familiar format, made its annual appearance (see pages 122-134).

CHEVY CAMARO.
THE HUGGER.

Take a look. Here's the shape that turns heads and quickens heartbeats. Chevy Camaro. The Hugger. Camaro is a car that helps recapture the fun and excitement and challenge of driving. That's the way it's been since the first Camaro took to the road back in September of '66.

Over the years we've developed several different styles of Camaro excitement. It all starts with the fun of a Sport Coupe. Then, there's the stylish roadability of the Rally Sport. You can sense the excite-ment that lies hidden just beneath the elegance and comfort of the Berlinetta, or take the full, high-voltage charge that comes from Camaro Z28, the maximum Camaro.

It's all here for those who enjoy the thrill of reaching out and grip-ping the wheel, leaning back and

2   *On cover: Camaro Z28 shown in red orange.*

looking out across the classic windswept hood of The Hugger.

If you're looking for the excitement and unmistakable good looks that have attracted more than two million Americans, you need look no further. They are here. In Chevy Camaro.

A WORD ABOUT THIS CATALOG

We have tried to make this catalog as comprehensive and factual as possible. And we hope you find it helpful. However, since the time of printing, some of the information you'll find here may have been updated. Also, some of the equipment shown or described throughout this catalog is available at extra cost. Your dealer has details and, before ordering, you should ask him to bring you up to date.

The right is reserved to make changes at any time, without notice, in prices, colors, materials, equipment, specifications and models, and to discontinue models. Check with your Chevrolet dealer for complete information.

Camaro Z28 shown in black, Rally Sport shown in bright blue metallic, Berlinetta shown in red and Sport Coupe shown in bright yellow. 3

5.7 Liter 4-Bbl. (350 Cu. In.) Dual resonators/tailpipes. 15" x 7" body-color wheels. Special springs. Special shocks/front and
V8 (5.0 Liter 4-Bbl. (305 Cu.   rear stabilizers.
In.) in California).

Camaro Z28 shown in black with available aluminum wheels,
Custom interior and roof drip moldings.

Z 28 FOR 1980.
THE MAXIMUM
CAMARO.

This is Camaro Z28. It's a very special machine for people who are dedicated to one ideal: performance. Z28 is the Camaro for people not satisfied with the ordinary.

Z28 starts with a potent 350-cubic-inch V8. Its impressive power and torque output is then teamed up with a four-speed gearbox (305-cubic-inch V8 and automatic transmission required in California) and a 3.08 rear end. Z28 announces itself with a unique exhaust note from the standard dual resonators.

Chevy takes this highly respected powertrain and matches it with a tough performance suspension specially designed for the Z28. It includes hefty front and rear stabilizer bars and special heavy-duty shocks and springs.

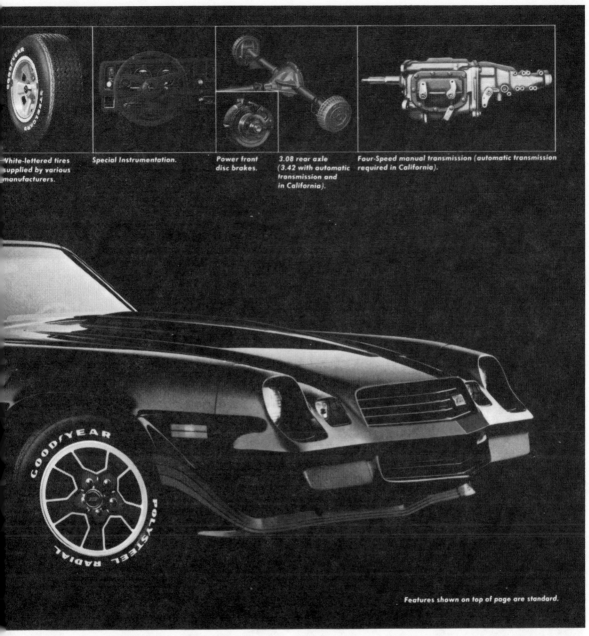

White-lettered tires supplied by various manufacturers.

Special Instrumentation.

Power front disc brakes.

3.08 rear axle (3.42 with automatic transmission and in California).

Four-Speed manual transmission (automatic transmission required in California).

Features shown on top of page are standard.

Z28 is also one of the best-dressed cars on the street with a rear spoiler, front air dam, rear fender flares, white-lettered steel-belted radials and a bold new Z28 stripe and body-color grille.

Inside you can grip the large rim sport steering wheel and watch the kind of gages a driver needs, like a tach, voltmeter, temperature gage, and electric clock—all standard.

For 1980 Z28 boasts new technical features like a functional solenoid-operated air-intake hood scoop and new, functional fender exhaust ports. Together they are designed to improve air recirculation under the hood.

Woven into this is the road-hugging heart of an American classic—Chevy Camaro. The Hugger. Drive a Z28. The Camaro for people who demand more than the ordinary.

CAMARO BERLINETTA.

Berlinetta continues the quiet sensation. It's a luxurious Camaro. Quiet. Comfortable. Yet, with a blend of sport styling and lean lines that puts a different accent on luxury.

A Berlinetta starts with Camaro excitement. With a Camaro's love for the road. There's a responsive new 3.8 Liter (229 Cu. In.) V6 engine. A sleekly styled body that smoothly parts the air. Then come the standard features that make a Berlinetta a Berlinetta.

Deluxe insulating package. Outside noise is reduced with an inner roof layer of sound-absorbing material, covered by a thick soft headliner that further reduces noise distractions. Bottom door seals are then added to help dampen vibration, wind and road noise.

Balanced riding ease. Berlinetta irons out bumps with a suspension package all its own that includes specially valved shocks, new front springs and relocated engine mounts.

Lush interior comfort. Tailored fabrics and deep foam comfort only start the list of distinctive features. There's also a bright-accented Gage Package with tachometer, voltmeter, temperature gage and electric clock as standard equipment in all Berlinettas.

Sophisticated exterior appointments. New bright grille and new wire wheel covers are an extra Berlinetta refinement this year. In addition, the white-stripe steel-belted radial ply tires, black-accented rocker panels and Berlinetta identification on the front end, trunk lid and rear roof panels all contribute to the Berlinetta's long, low, lean and luxurious lines.

Berlinetta—truly an extraordinary Camaro.

6 Camaro Berlinetta shown in red with available Style Trim Group.

Camaro Berlinetta interior shown in camel with available Custom cloth, automatic transmission, power windows and power door-lock system.

7

CAMARO RALLY SPORT.

It's an escape from the routine. With its unique body paint scheme and rear spoiler, the Rally Sport is a distinctive blend of style and performance.

The Rally Sport stands out from the crowd with its unmistakable special exterior color pattern. Dark contrasting hood. Matching dark paint on the forward part of the roof. They're color-keyed in black, dark blue, charcoal or dark brown to accent the body color you choose. With a new blacked-out grille, rocker panels, color-keyed Rally wheels, Sport mirrors and a new three-tone striping package, and the world knows it's looking at something special.

The Rally Sport is special under that distinctive styling, too. Standard is a new 3.8 Liter (229 Cu. In.) V6 engine. And it hugs the road with a set of steel-belted radial ply tires, front stabilizer bar, power steering and specially tuned shock absorbers, all standard.

Camaro Rally Sport. It's anything but routine to drive.

Camaro Rally Sport shown in bright blue metallic with available removable glass roof panels, white-stripe tires and Custom interior.

CAMARO SPORT COUPE.

For those who love just the pure pleasure of heading for the open road, there's the Camaro Sport Coupe.

Everything's there to make driving fun . . . and affordable. From the plush interior with full foam bucket seats and cut-pile carpeting to the new 3.8 Liter (229 Cu. In.) V6 engine. Outside, there's the sleek good looks and sporty flair that's become a Camaro hallmark.

And Camaro rides as good as it looks. With a balanced suspension that includes a front stabilizer bar, power steering, steel-belted radial ply tires and multi-leaf rear springs. All contribute to the Sport Coupe's ability to hug the road.

The Sport Coupe. Fun. Affordable. Camaro.

Camaro Sport Coupe shown in silver with available Sport mirrors, color-keyed Rally wheels, steel-belted radial ply white-lettered tires and roof drip moldings.

CAMARO STANDARD FEATURES.

1. Power steering. Puts you in touch with the road with little effort.

2. Center floor console. Color-keyed to match interior. Includes floor shift lever.

3. Front disc/ rear drum brakes. A self-adjusting system. Fade-resistant front disc brakes have audible wear sensors to let you know when to replace linings.

4. Visible ball joint wear indicators. Located on front suspension lower control arms for visual check of ball joint wear.

5. Inner fenders. Inner shield on front and rear fenders helps provide road splash protection.

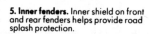

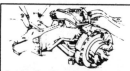

Front coil and rear leaf suspension. Resilient coil springs at each front wheel and multi-leaf rear wheel springs are computer-selected to match each model and equipment weight.

Front stabilizer bar. Helps add stability to reduce body lean during sharp turns.

High Energy Ignition. A solid-state system that eliminates points and ignition condenser and delivers a high-voltage spark that helps extend time between recommended tune-ups.

Steel-belted radial ply tires. Offer lower rolling resistance than conventional bias ply tires plus impressive traction.

DIMENSIONS (inches)

Exterior	All models
Wheelbase	108.0
Length (overall)	197.6
Width (overall)	74.5
Height (loaded)	49.2
Tread—front	61.3*
Tread—rear	60.0†

Interior	
Head Room—Front	37.2
Head Room—Rear	36.0
Leg Room—Front	43.9
Leg Room—Rear	28.4
Hip Room—Front	55.3
Hip Room—Rear	46.3
Shoulder Room—Front	56.7
Shoulder Room—Rear	54.4
Usable Luggage Capacity (cu. ft.)	7.1

*Berlinetta 61.6.
†Berlinetta 60.3.

A WORD ABOUT ENGINES

Chevrolets are equipped with GM-built engines produced by various divisions. Please refer to the Camaro Power Team Chart or see your dealer for details.

ENGINE SELECTION

3.8 LITER V6s

These engines are new for 1980 and standard on all models except the Z28. Two variations of a 3.8 Liter V6 are used, the 231-cu.-in. version in California and the 229-cu.-in. version standard in the remaining 49 states. Both feature a "V6" design that is light in weight. They deliver impressive power and quick, even response. Hydraulic valve lifters help provide a smooth and quiet flow of power. They're engines that deliver performance for today's kind of driving.

4.4 LITER V8

This available V8 includes short-stroke valve-in-head design and Dualjet carburetor which help provide good engine performance at all speed ranges. Also features a cast-iron cylinder block with full jacket cylinder cooling, a precision-balanced, cast-iron crankshaft, hydraulic valve lifters and exhaust valve rotators for even wear.

5.0 LITER V8

This available engine features short-stroke valve-in-head design and downdraft carburetor which help provide good engine performance at all speed ranges. You also get full jacket cylinder cooling, a precision-balanced crankshaft and hydraulic valve lifters.

5.7 LITER V8

The rugged Z28 powerplant has impressive low-speed torque for around-town cruising and is also very responsive on the highway.

LONG RECOMMENDED SERVICE INTERVALS
(Under normal driving conditions)

Engine Oil . . . . . .12 months or 7,500 miles
Oil Filter . . . . . . .12 months or 7,500 miles; every 15,000 miles thereafter
Spark Plugs . . . . .Up to 30,000 miles*
Chassis Lubrication . . . . .12 months or 7,500 miles
Automatic Transmission Fluid Change . . . . .100,000 miles
*22,500 miles with 4.4 Liter V8.

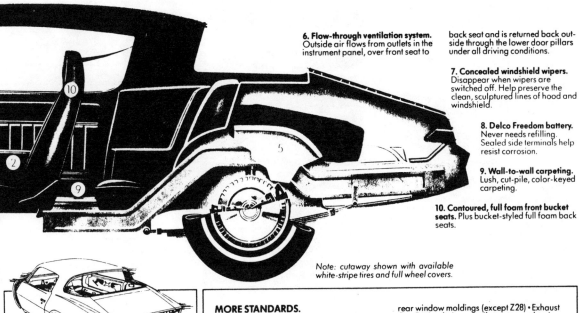

6. Flow-through ventilation system. Outside air flows from outlets in the instrument panel, over front seat to back seat and is returned back outside through the lower door pillars under all driving conditions.

7. Concealed windshield wipers. Disappear when wipers are switched off. Help preserve the clean, sculptured lines of hood and windshield.

8. Delco Freedom battery. Never needs refilling. Sealed side terminals help resist corrosion.

9. Wall-to-wall carpeting. Lush, cut-pile, color-keyed carpeting.

10. Contoured, full foam front bucket seats. Plus bucket-styled full foam back seats.

Note: cutaway shown with available white-stripe tires and full wheel covers.

Anti-corrosion measures. Precoated steel is used for reinforcement and underbody crossbars, and ventilated rocker panels are designed to permit good air circulation and water drainage to help guard against corrosion.

MORE STANDARDS.
Coolant recovery system • Delcotron generator with built-in solid-state regulator • Integral coil distributor cap helps protect coil from heat and moisture • Fuel vapor canister captures vapors from the carburetor as well as the fuel tank after engine shutdown for improved vapor recovery and emission control • Body by Fisher • Front and rear styling in resilient urethane • Body-colored front and rear bumper system • Bright windshield and full rear window moldings (except Z28) • Exhaust Gas Recirculation contributes to good emission control • New instrument panel pad and cluster styling • Soft-rim, vinyl-covered four-spoke sport steering wheel • Heater-defroster system • Catalytic converter • Double-wall construction that provides two layers of steel in doors, hood and deck lid • Deluxe color-keyed seat and shoulder belts.
For features standard on Berlinetta, Z28 and Rally Sport, see pages 4 through 9.

CAMARO POWER TEAMS

Engine	Ordering Code	Power Rating*	Displacement (cubic inches)	All Models Except Z28	Z28 Only	Three-Speed Manual (1)	Four-Speed Manual (1)	Automatic
ALL STATES EXCEPT CALIFORNIA								
3.8 Liter 2-Bbl. V6 (A)	LC3	115	229	Std.	NA	Std.	NA	EC
4.4 Liter 2-Bbl. V8 (B)	L39	120	267	EC(2)	NA	NA	NA	EC
5.0 Liter 4-Bbl. V8 (B)	LG4	155	305	EC(2)	NA	NA	EC	EC
5.7 Liter 4-Bbl. V8 (A)	LM1	190	350	NA	Std.	NA	Std.	EC
CALIFORNIA ONLY (with California Emission Requirements)								
3.8 Liter 2-Bbl. V6 (C)	LD5	110	231	Std.	NA	NA	NA	EC
5.0 Liter 4-Bbl. V8 (B)	LG4	155	305	EC(2)	NA	NA	NA	EC
5.0 Liter 4-Bbl. V8 (B)	LG4	165	305	NA	Std.	NA	NA	EC

*S.A.E. net horsepower as installed.   Std.–Standard.   NA–Not Available.
 EC–Available at extra cost.
(1) With floor-mounted shift control.
(2) Power brakes (RPO J50) required.
(A) PRODUCED BY GM-CHEVROLET MOTOR DIVISION.
(B) PRODUCED BY GM-CHEVROLET MOTOR DIVISION AND GM OF CANADA.
(C) PRODUCED BY GM-BUICK MOTOR DIVISION.

SAFETY FEATURES
OCCUPANT PROTECTION
Seat belts with push-button buckles for all passenger positions • Two front combination seat and inertia reel shoulder belts for driver (with reminder light and buzzer) and right front passenger • Energy-absorbing steering column • Passenger guard door locks • Safety door latches and stamped steel hinges • Folding seat back latches • Energy-absorbing padded instrument panel and front seat back tops • Laminated windshield • Safety armrests.
ACCIDENT AVOIDANCE
Side marker lights and reflectors • Parking lamps that illuminate with headlamps • Four-way hazard warning flasher • Lane-change feature in direction signal control • Backup lights • Windshield defrosters, washer and dual-speed wipers • Wideview inside mirror (vinyl-edged, shatter-resistant glass and deflecting support) • Outside rearview mirror • Dual master cylinder brake system with warning light • Starter safety switch • Dual-action safety hood latch.
ANTI-THEFT
Anti-theft ignition key reminder buzzer • Anti-theft steering column lock.

CAMARO AVAILABLE OPTIONS.

1. Air conditioning. Provides cooling and ventilating functions with convenient, easy-to-operate controls.

2. Sound systems. Produced by Delco to General Motors quality standards. Many systems to select from, including: AM/FM/Citizens Band radio with power antenna, AM/FM stereo/Citizens Band radio with power antenna, AM/FM stereo radio with stereo 8-track tape, AM/FM stereo radio with stereo cassette tape and AM/FM stereo radio with digital clock display. See back cover for a complete list of available sound equipment.

3. Gage Package with tachometer. Consists of electric clock, tachometer, voltmeter and temperature gage. Standard on Z28 and Berlinetta.

4. Automatic transmission. Shifts for you in three forward gears; can also be shifted manually.

5. Automatic speed control. Holds a steady speed without pressure on the accelerator. Disengages automatically when brake pedal is depressed.

Available with power brakes and automatic transmission only.

6. Comfortilt steering wheel. Adjusts to six different positions for most comfortable driving angle and for easy entry and exiting.

7. Custom styled wheels. Available on Sport Coupe and Rally Sport. Not available on Z28 or Berlinetta.

8. Aluminum wheels. Brand-new lightweight additions to Camaro this year, available in 15" x 7" on the Z28 and 14" x 7" on Berlinetta, Rally Sport and Sport Coupe.

9. Full wheel covers. Stainless steel to resist dirt and corrosion. Available for Sport Coupe only.

10. Power windows. Raise or lower windows at a touch of a button.

11. Power door lock system. This convenient feature locks both doors with the flick of a switch on either door.

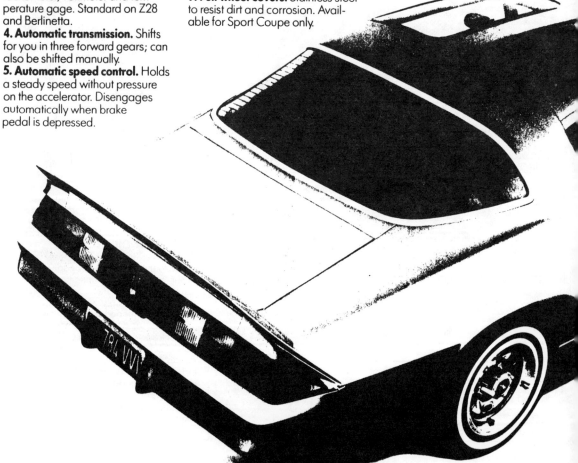

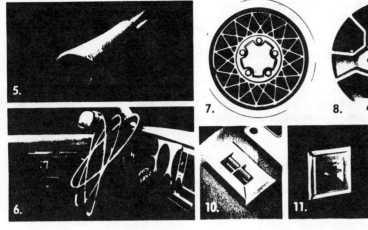

Other options available shown here include: **removable glass roof panels** which can be taken off and stored away with ease on sunny days and moonlit nights, **electric rear window defogger** with a wire grid that helps clear window of fog and mist, **Sport mirrors** that help increase rear visibility (standard on Z28, Berlinetta and Rally Sport), **rear spoiler** that adds even more rear styling (standard on Rally Sport and Z28) and **color-keyed Rally wheels,** include bright trim rings and wheel opening cutouts plus hubcaps. Standard on Rally Sport, available Sport Coupe.

The GM Continuous Protection Plan. Offers service protection in addition to that provided by GM's new vehicle limited warranty. Ask your dealer about it. Coverage available only in the U.S.A. and Canada for the 1980 model year.

Camaro Sport Coupe shown in bright blue metallic with available removable glass roof panels, Sport mirrors, rear spoiler, electric rear window defogger, color-keyed Rally wheels and white-stripe tires.

A WORD ABOUT ASSEMBLY, COMPONENTS AND OPTIONAL EQUIPMENT IN THESE CHEVROLETS.

The Chevrolets described in this catalog are assembled at facilities of General Motors Corporation operated by the GM Assembly Division. These vehicles incorporate thousands of different components produced by various divisions of General Motors and by various suppliers to General Motors. From time to time during the manufacturing process, it may be necessary, in order to meet public demand for particular vehicles or equipment, or to meet federally mandated emissions, safety and fuel economy requirements, or for other reasons, to produce Chevrolet products with different components or differently sourced components than initially scheduled. All such components have been approved for use in Chevrolet products and will provide the quality performance associated with the Chevrolet name.

With respect to extra cost optional equipment, make certain you specify the type of equipment you desire on your vehicle when ordering it from your dealer. Some options may be unavailable when your car is built. Your dealer receives advice regarding current availability of options. You may ask the dealer for this information. GM also requests the dealer to advise you if an option you ordered is unavailable. We suggest you verify that your car includes the optional equipment you ordered or, if there are changes, that they are acceptable to you.

REASONS TO BUY CAMARO

• EXCITING, SPORTY, STREAMLINED APPEARANCE.
• FOUR DISTINCT SPORT PERSONALITIES.
• SPIRITED PERFORMANCE FROM A SELECTION OF V6 AND V8 ENGINES.
• DRIVER-ORIENTED, COCKPIT-LIKE INTERIOR
WITH HIGHLY CONTOURED FRONT BUCKET SEATS AND FLOOR SHIFT.
• QUALITY ENGINEERED AND DESIGNED FOR VALUE.

BUILD YOUR OWN CAMARO

MODELS
☐ Berlinetta   ☐ Z28   ☐ Rally Sport   ☐ Sport Coupe

COLORS (See chart on page 10 for color availabilities and combinations.)
Exterior color _____
Second color (on Rally Sport only) _____
Interior color _____
Upholstery (cloth or vinyl) _____

ENGINES (See chart on page 13 for engine/transmission availability.)
☐ 3.8 Liter 2-Bbl. (229 Cu. In.) V6—Std.
☐ 4.4 Liter 2-Bbl. (267 Cu. In.) V8—Avail.
☐ 5.0 Liter 4-Bbl. (305 Cu. In.) V8—Avail.
☐ 5.7 Liter 4-Bbl. (350 Cu. In.) V8—Std. Z28†

TRANSMISSIONS
☐ Automatic (Avail.)*   ☐ Three-Speed manual (Std.)†   ☐ Four-Speed manual (Avail.)†

AVAILABLE OPTIONS

(Not all options are available on all models. See your dealer for
up-to-date ordering information and specific model/option availability.)

☐ Power windows.
☐ Air conditioning.
☐ Power brakes.
☐ Electric clock.
☐ Comfortilt steering wheel.
☐ Automatic speed control.
☐ Power door lock system.
☐ Electric rear window defogger.
☐ Tinted glass.
☐ Auxiliary lighting.
☐ Gage Package with tachometer (includes electric clock, voltmeter and engine temperature gage). Standard on Z28 and Berlinetta.
☐ Interior Decor/Quiet Sound Group.
☐ Intermittent windshield wiper system.
☐ Custom interior.

MOLDINGS AND TRIM
☐ Door edge guards.
☐ Roof drip moldings.
☐ Body side moldings.
☐ Rear spoiler.
☐ Style Trim Group.

SOUND EQUIPMENT
☐ AM radio.
☐ AM/FM radio.
☐ AM/FM/Citizens Band radio with power antenna.
☐ AM/FM stereo/Citizens Band radio with power antenna.
☐ AM/FM stereo radio.
☐ AM radio with 8-track stereo tape.
☐ AM/FM stereo radio with 8-track stereo tape.
☐ AM/FM stereo radio with stereo cassette tape.
☐ AM/FM stereo radio with digital clock display.
☐ Rear seat speaker.
☐ Windshield antenna.
☐ Power antenna.

WHEELS AND WHEEL COVERS
☐ Aluminum wheels.
☐ Full wheel covers.
☐ Color-keyed Rally wheels.
☐ Custom styled wheels.

TIRES
☐ P205/75R-14 steel-belted radial ply white-stripe.
☐ P205/75R-14 steel-belted radial ply white-lettered.

MISCELLANEOUS
☐ Removable glass roof panels.
☐ Performance axle ratio.
☐ Color-keyed floor mats, front and rear.
☐ Dual horns.
☐ Sport mirrors, LH remote and RH manual.
☐ Heavy-duty cooling.
☐ Adjustable driver's seat back.
☐ Stowaway spare tire.
☐ Sport suspension.
☐ Heavy-duty battery.
☐ Limited slip differential.

*Required in California.
†Not available in California.

The last model year for the ten and one-half year-old body style was a quiet one. Chevrolet was working toward introduction of the new downsized Camaro and wasn't really trying to capture a great deal of new buyers that year.

The Z28 was tamed a little more for 1981; the base engine became the 5.0 liter (305 cid) in all 50 states, although the 5.7 liter (350 cid) engine was still an option. Horsepower wasn't even listed in the sales literature. The four-speed manual transmission was standard, with the automatic optional on the 5 liter and required on the 5.7 liter versions. The 5.0 liter could be ordered in any Camaro, not just the Z28.

But engines alone did not make the Z28; the other goodies were still there: F-41 suspension, solenoid-activated cold air intake scoop, dual exhausts and resonators, power front disc brakes, GR70x15 raised-letter radial tires mounted on 15x7 inch body-color Trans Am wheels, full instrumentation, dual sport mirrors and, of course, the graphics.

The striping continued from last year; fluorescent tricolor stripes extended from the rear of the doors forward, narrowing as they dipped down in front of the wheels to run along the lower front lip of the air dam. On each side, the stripes ended in the letters "Z28." The same tricolor motif was carried on the grille and fuel filler door badges and on the pinstripe that ran across the back between the tail-lights and the spoiler, as well as on the pinstripe that ran around the upper edge of the hood scoop. The

block letters "AIR INDUCTION" were affixed to both sides of the scoop. Maybe the 1981 Z28 didn't have the gut-wrenching power of the early models, but it could still get the juices flowing and give you the urge to drive.

The model lineup for 1981 was missing the Rally Sport. Besides the Z28, the Berlinetta and the Sport Coupe were the only other choices. The Berlinetta interior took on a more formal appearance with subdued hues of cloth and vinyl.

Engine availability remained the same as for 1980; the base engine was the 3.8 liter V-6, although the California version was listed as two cubic inches larger in displacement than the 49-state: 231 versus 229. The 4.4 liter V-8 was available in all states except California and the same 5.0 liter engine that came in the Z28 was available in all models, minus the cold-air induction system.

The Z28 enjoyed wide appeal in its first 14 years. Including the 43,272 Zs sold in 1981, 310,9903 had been produced since its inception. A total of 2,449,579 Camaros were built during that same time. Throughout the three body styles and numerous model designations, one constant remained: Camaros offered a pleasing, sporty car in a 2+2 configuration that brought a measure of automotive enthusiasm to those who owned them.

For its final year, Chevrolet issued an unusual, over-size Camaro catalogue (see pages 136-143).

THE HUGGER. PERSONALITY, PLUS.

Sleek and crisp. Show-stopping good looks. An unmistakable zest
for hugging the road and capturing the heart. And a flair for moving through life with
style. That's the 1981 Camaro. It's got all the characteristics that make one
well-rounded personal car.

It's practical to drive, with a wide selection of engine and transmission teams,
practical to own with new features and engineering improvements. Since its first
introduction, Chevy engineers have continued to upgrade Camaro to its present level of
roadability and performance. And for '81 they've added standard power brakes,
a standard compact spare tire for increased luggage capacity and the Computer
Command Control system which aids in good gas mileage* and emissions control.

All this captured in three
stylish Camaro models designed to satisfy your own unique spirit. Choose from
the Sport Coupe, the quietly sensational Berlinetta, or the performance
and excitement of the Z28. Each is complete with Camaro's fine
engineering and tailored features, yet each has its own distinct
personality. Just like you.

For a closer look, turn the page.

A WORD ABOUT THIS CATALOG.   We have tried to make this catalog as comprehensive and factual as possible and we hope you find it helpful.
However, since the time of printing, some of the information you'll find here may have been updated. Also, some of the equipment shown or
described throughout this catalog is available at extra cost. Your dealer has details and, before ordering, you should ask him to bring you up to
date.

The right is reserved to make changes at any time, without notice, in prices, colors, materials, equipment, specifications and models. Check with
your Chevrolet dealer for complete information.

*For Camaro EPA estimated mileage, check the wall poster displayed at your Chevrolet dealer's showroom, or ask for an EPA mileage sheet to take
home with you.

Camaro Berlinetta.

Litho in U.S.A.   July, 1980   3971

BERLINETTA. THE QUIETLY SENSATIONAL HUGGER.

Berlinetta wears luxury with the ease of a car that's been doing it for a long time. Sensational but not extravagant. Refined but not expensive. A car distinctly its own in any setting.

Perhaps Berlinetta's most special quality is the way it reduces exterior noises. In fact, it's still the quietest Camaro of them all. This is achieved with the addition of the standard Quiet Sound Group which reduces outside noises with an inner roof layer of sound-absorbing materials and with the inside roof covering of soft, foam-backed headlining. There are also bottom door seals that help dampen vibration, wind and road sounds. So, as you can see, Berlinetta takes quiet very seriously.

The Custom trim level adds to the overall comfort with carpeted lower doors and soft, contoured bucket seats—standard only on the Berlinetta. Also standard is special lighting inside and special instrumentation, including a tachometer, voltmeter, temperature gage and electric clock.

Other Berlinetta distinctions include a special paint and striping treatment to emphasize the sporty, sculptured lines. White-stripe steel-belted radials are standard, as are wire wheel covers. And a new anti-theft Wheel Cover Locking Package is optional for the wire wheels.

Camaro Berlinetta. So easy to attain.

Camaro Berlinetta.

5

Z28. PERFORMANCE MADE AFFORDABLE.

Z28. It's tempting. To the one who wants performance. To the one who wants affordability. Or both. Together they represent an impressive combination. Performance that's affordable. At no sacrifice to the Camaro legend.

Z28 sizzles with the excitement that lies beneath and beyond the grip of its sports steering wheel, the design of its tasteful graphics— and the feeling you get when you team up the standard four-speed manual transmission with the 5.0 Liter V8 engine and put it through the paces meant for a car such as this. Even the special sport suspension says this one was meant to command the road.

It's all part of the Z28 tradition that boasts a front air dam and fender opening flares, front fender louvers, hood scoop and decal, rear spoiler, and raised white-lettered tires with body-colored sport wheels. Inside, it's just as tempting with contoured bucket seats and full instrumentation. Camaro Z28. Let it loose.

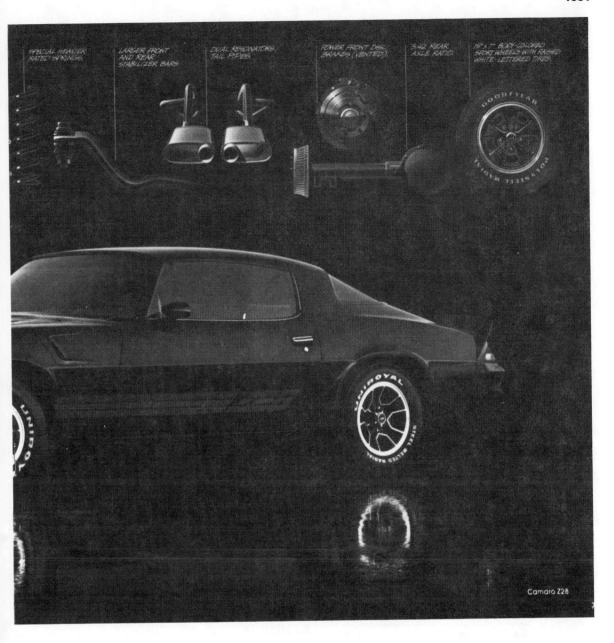

Camaro Z28

CAMARO POWER TEAMS.

ENGINE	Ordering Code	Displacement (cu. in.)	Sport Coupe & Berlinetta	Z28	3-speed Manual (1)	4-speed Manual (1)	Automatic
ALL STATES EXCEPT CALIFORNIA							
3.8 Liter 2-Bbl. V6 (A)	LC3	229	Std.	NA	Std.	NA	Opt.
4.4 Liter 2-Bbl. V8 (B)	L39	267	Opt.	NA	NA	NA	Opt.
5.0 Liter 4-Bbl. V8 (B)	LG4	305	Opt.	Std.	NA	Opt. (Std. Z28)	Opt. (NA Z28)
5.7 Liter 4-Bbl. V8 (A)	LM1	350	NA	Opt.	NA	NA	Opt.
CALIFORNIA ONLY							
3.8 Liter 2-Bbl. V6 (C)	LD5	231	Std.	NA	NA	NA	Opt.
5.0 Liter 4-Bbl. V8 (B)	LG4	305	Opt.	Std.	NA	Opt. (Std. Z28)	Opt. (NA Z28)
5.7 Liter 4-Bbl. V8 (A)	LM1	350	NA	Opt.	NA	NA	Opt.

Std.—Standard. NA—Not Available. Opt.—Optional. (1) With floor-mounted shift control. PRODUCED BY GM: (A) CHEVROLET MOTOR DIVISION. (B) CHEVROLET MOTOR DIVISION; GM OF CANADA. (C) BUICK MOTOR DIVISION.

LONG RECOMMENDED SERVICE INTERVALS.*

Engine Oil . . .12 months or 7,500 miles
Oil Filter . . . . .12 months, or 7,500 miles; every 15,000 miles thereafter
Spark Plugs . . . . .30,000 miles
Chassis Lubrication . . . . . . .12 months or 7,500 miles
Automatic Transmission Fluid Change . . Every 100,000 miles

*See Owner's Manual for conditions requiring more frequent intervals.

EXTERIOR DIMENSIONS.

Wheelbase	108.0
Length (overall)	197.6
Width (overall)	74.5
Height (loaded)	50.1
Tread—Front	61.3
Tread—Rear	60.0

ENGINE SELECTION.

3.8 LITER V6s.

These engines are standard on Sport Coupe and Berlinetta for 1981. Two variations of a 3.8 Liter V6 are used, the 231-cu.-in. version in California and the 229-cu.-in. version standard in the remaining 49 states. Both feature a "V6" design that is light in weight. They deliver impressive power and quick, even response.

4.4 LITER V8.

This optional V8 includes short-stroke design and Dualjet carburetor which help provide good engine performance at all speed ranges. It also features a cast-iron cylinder block with full jacket cylinder cooling, a precision-balanced, cast-iron crankshaft, hydraulic valve lifters and exhaust valve rotators for even wear.

5.0 LITER V8.

This optional engine (standard on Z28) features short-stroke valve-in-head design. You also get full jacket cylinder cooling, a precision-balanced crankshaft and hydraulic valve lifters.

5.7 LITER V8.

This performance-minded Z28 optional powerplant delivers impressive low-speed torque for around-town cruising and is also very responsive on the highway.

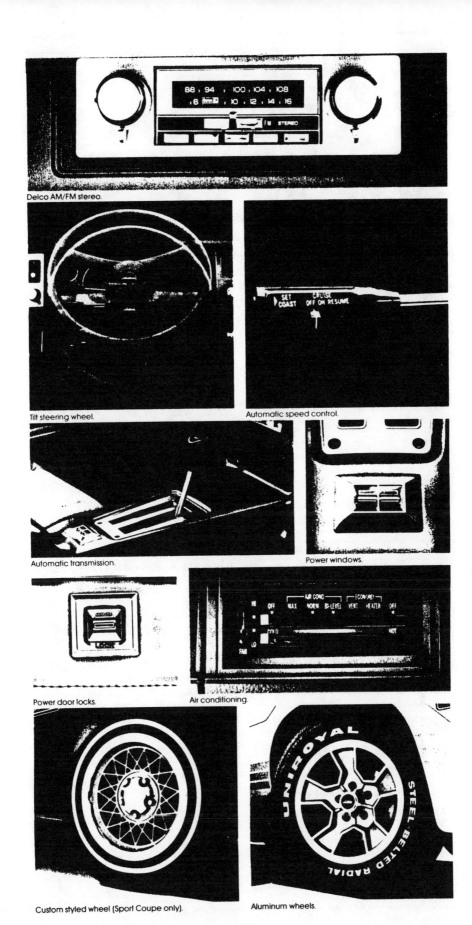

Delco AM/FM stereo.

Tilt steering wheel.

Automatic speed control.

Automatic transmission.

Power windows.

Power door locks.

Air conditioning.

Custom styled wheel (Sport Coupe only).

Aluminum wheels.

SOURCE BOOKS!

1. GTO (Bonsall)
2. Firebird (Bonsall)
3. AMX (Campbell)
4. Chrysler 300 (Bonsall)
5. Chevelle SS (Lehwald)
6. 4-4-2 (Casteele)
7. Charger (Shields)
8. Javelin (Campbell)
9. Corvette, 1953-1967 (Steffen)
10. Nova SS (Lehwald)
11. Barracuda/Challenger (Shields)
12. Roadrunner (Shields)
13. Corvette, 1968-1982 (Steffen)
14. Cougar 1967-1976 (Bonsall)
15. Trans Am, 1967-1981 (Bonsall)
16. El Camino (Lehwald)
17. Big Chevys, 1955-1970 (Lehwald)
18. Big Pontiacs, 1955-1970 (Bonsall)
19. Duster/Demon (Shields)
20. Ranchero (Ackerson)

21. Mid-Size Fords/Mercs (Ackerson)
22. Porsche 911/912 (Miller)
23. Buick Gran Sports (Zavitz)
24. Shelby, Cobras and Mustangs (Ackerson)
25. Mid-Size Dodges (Shields)
26. Ferraris of the Seventies (Ackerson)
27. Z/28 (Collins)
28. Lamborghini (Ackerson)
29. Big Fords & Mercs (Shields)
30. Jaguar XK-E (Sass)*
31. Mustang (Ackerson)*

CLASSIC SOURCE BOOKS

1. Mark Lincolns (Bonsall)
2. Eldorados (Bonsall)*

*To be published later in 1984.

All volumes $12.95 each